Mother

Memoirs of Struggle & Strength

Brenda M. Doyle
Melanie Faye
Nancy Garrow
Kathy Honickman
Jennifer Walcott
Ellen O'Donnell Walters

DEMETER

Mother Load

Memoirs of Struggle & Strength

Brenda M. Doyle, Melanie Faye, Nancy Garrow,
Kathy Honickman, Jennifer Walcott, Ellen O'Donnell Walters

Demeter Press
2546 10th Line
Bradford, Ontario
Canada, L3Z 3L3
Tel: 289-383-0134
Email: info@demeterpress.org
Website: www.demeterpress.org

Demeter Press logo based on the sculpture "Demeter" by Maria-Luise Bodirsky
www.keramik-atelier.bodirsky.de

Printed and Bound in Canada

Cover artwork: Mindy Johnstone
Cover design and typesetting: Michelle Pirovich
Proof reading: Jena Woodhouse

Library and Archives Canada Cataloguing in Publication
Title: Mother Load : Memoirs of Struggle & Strength / by Nancy Garrow, Jennifer Walcott, Melanie Faye, Brenda M. Doyle, Kathy Honickman, and Ellen O'Donnell Walters.
Names: Garrow, Nancy, author.
Description: Includes bibliographical references.
Identifiers: Canadiana 20220261393 | ISBN 9781772584103 (softcover)
Subjects: LCSH: Motherhood. | LCSH: Mothers, Biography. | LCSH: Mother and child. | LCSH: Motherhood, Literary collections. | LCSH: Mothers, Literary collections. | LCSH: Mother and child, Literary collections. | LCGFT: Creative nonfiction. | LCGFT: Autobiographies. | LCGFT: Literature.
Classification: LCC PS8237.M64 G37 2022 | DDC C810.8/035252, dc23

  The publisher gratefully acknowledges the support of the Government of Canada

Funded by the Government of Canada

Prologue

Behind all your stories is always your mother's story,
Because hers is where yours begins

— from **Mitch Albom**, *For One More Day*

Contents

Introduction

**Brenda M. Doyle, Melanie Faye, Nancy Garrow,
Kathy Honickman, Jennifer Walcott, Ellen O'Donnell Walters**

Three years ago, we six women met through the Academy for Lifelong Learning of Toronto and developed friendships over time and a strong bond through memoir writing.

The original theme for our writing was "Momma, we hardly knew you," but that early theme shifted as we wrote about other important mothering relationships as well. Over time, we became individually, and as a group, stronger, developing greater capacities for understanding the past. The scope of our collection grew with mutual encouragement to stretch and go deeper. The pieces in this book are the result of the ongoing give and take, support and critique, deepening trust, and friendship that became the grounding for this collection.

We painted pictures of mothers, grandmothers, aunts, sisters, daughters, and friends. Grief, anger, and loss are also here as well as insights, perspective, and gratitude. Moreover, the silence in these relationships has been highlighted: what was assumed, what was unquestioned or undiscussable, and what was too shameful or painful to be put into words.

The pieces are in the form of memoir, inner monologue, poetry, and short story. They let readers in on some of the realities of mothering from the 1940s to the early 2000s, some of which seem barely recognizable in 2022.

This kaleidoscope of courageous, sometimes raw, sometimes loving, narratives bring to the surface the tensions that haunt mothering relationships across generations. In their telling lies hope for better.

1. Nancy Garrow

Nancy came to writing late in life after years of pondering the memories of so many years. She was encouraged by the Memoir Writing and Reading Workshop at the Academy for Lifelong Learning Toronto.

Nancy's life story started with a contented and calm childhood, then time spent raising a family of three, finding a career in her forties in the legal world all while immersing herself in many volunteer opportunities. Traumas along the way led her to reflect deeply on her life journey.

Now with a grown family and six grandchildren and the time to enjoy retirement, she finds satisfaction in writing her memoirs. To share stories with her family, both the happy and tragic ones, is hopefully a gift to the next generation.

Rosalind

The name comes from Shakespeare's *As You Like It*. Rosalind was considered one of Shakespeare's most delightful heroines, an independent minded, strong-willed, good-hearted and terribly clever young woman. And like Shakespeare's heroine, my mother Rosalind's life also held a big secret and a lie that for the longest time shaped me.

Born in 1911, my mother Rosalind's early life was one of calm, privilege, and richness. She was the third of four children, all named for literary characters, which says much about the environment that shaped her childhood. Music, literature, and other arts filled their elegant Toronto home.

How Rosalind settled on classical ballet as her passion is somewhat of a serendipitous story. By the age of sixteen, she was bored with school and was drawn to dance. After an uneventful start at one dance studio, she saw an advertisement in the newspaper for a Russian studio and on a whim signed up. Dimitri, the owner, was a tough taskmaster but saw the potential in Rosalind. Her parents encouraged her. As a seventeen-year-old, she was amazed and delighted by their support and the trust they had in Dimitri and his wife, Leontina, two recent immigrants, to guide her career. She thrived and thus began a ten-year adventure changing the trajectory of her life. She danced classical ballet professionally in Toronto, Montreal, and eventually London, England.

In 1934, as she embarked on the London phase of her career, she was interviewed for a newspaper article in the *Toronto Star*. The discovery of this article so many years later, with actual quotes in her own voice, still gives me goosebumps and such admiration that at the young age of twenty-three she was brave and fearless and so confident in her future.

TORONTO GIRL CROSSES SEA - BALLET RUSSE HER AMBITION:

She is quoted:

I don't know how I'll live. Just now I feel like I'd like to be some place where I could be quiet and have my own friends when working hours are over.

Dancing is the most healthy exercise you can ever have. I have never been sick a day since I began.

I should say it was hard work but I loved it.

By this time, she had been to New York to study under Michel Fokine, the famous Russian choreographer, perfecting a solo from *The Firebird*. She had many accolades in newspaper reviews of dance performances in both Toronto and Montreal. More rave reviews followed from her four-year career in London, England.

Rosalind, *The Firebird*, 1934

But life has its chapters, and this chapter in Rosalind's life ended in 1938 as war loomed in Europe, and she was encouraged to come home. It must have been a very difficult decision. Still single at the age of twenty-seven, there were expectations from her traditional family to settle down and get married.

Beautiful, sophisticated, cultured, and full of the experiences of her career living abroad, she had many suitors. The fact that she was swept off her feet soon after returning to Canada by a handsome stockbroker who looked a lot like a movie star is not hard to believe. Within three months of meeting, they were married in 1938. She looked stunning in the wedding photographs in a short white dress and wonderful white flower in her hair.

Shortly after their marriage, my father joined the army. He came home occasionally on leave. My mother moved home to live with her recently widowed mother and her older sister, Sylvia. In this cozy environment, my sister was born in 1941, and I in 1943. Envisaging a home of three women taking care of two little girls always brings warm and loving thoughts to mind. I did indeed also have a truly privileged start in life.

My earliest memories are of the house we moved to when my father came home in 1945—a lovely leafy neighbourhood with children bursting out of every house on the block. Later, my younger brother arrived, completing our family of five. Mom excelled at homemaking, and I have vivid recollections of her cooking delicious meals and sewing beautiful dresses for my sister and me. A favourite was a pink felt skirt adorned with an appliqued sequined poodle, worn with a crinoline.

We spent many hours putting on shows, delving into the magical costume box filled with tutus and ethnic outfits from my mother's dance career. I recall that when Mom would take us to a live performance of the Sadlers Wells company in Toronto in the 1950s, if *The Firebird* had been on the program, she would count the number of fouettés the ballerina executed and say, "Well, Fokine made me do two more"—a poignant memory of her dance career so long ago.

Mom was always there. She didn't drive a car. We had a maid in the early years, but Mom was always busy with us and with keeping a warm and inviting home for everyone.

She made friends with the neighbourhood mothers, and they would often meet for coffee in the morning after we had gone to school. Those friendships must have been so important to her.

My mother's connection with her sister, Syl, was very tight. They were a duo, spending many hours together sewing, gardening, drinking tea, or just running errands. It was a dramatic change from her dazzling dance career with international travel to a stay-at-home mother with three children and a distant husband.

Where my father was is a blur. Yes, he lived with us, went to work every day, but mostly we were told to be quiet when he came home. He was a shadow to me in many ways. And I feared his temper, so mostly kept out of his way. He never spent time with me. No stories read before bed. No effort to help with school or sports. The mood at home was a divided one. My father provided, and my mother made everything calm and warm. My father's temper was to be managed and kept at bay as much as possible. The dinner table, where we had a formal dinner every night, could become a battle ground. My sister would sometimes bait my father. Mom would try to intervene in a conciliatory manner, and my brother and I would stay as quiet as mice. Sometimes my father's rage would end with him pounding his fist on the table and storming off. But Mom never raised her voice with him. I never heard a cross word between them.

Mom loved her garden. She was a champion golfer and volunteered at the hospital, making her days busy. She and my father had a very active social life, with parties, travel, and golf events.

She had an incredible style and a stunning wardrobe with designer dresses and beautiful hats. Sitting in her bedroom watching her get dressed to go out to a party, putting on her makeup, and doing her hair in a French twist fascinated me. She loved to get up and dance at parties; the Charleston was a favourite. She had a fabulous flapper dress, beaded and sequined.

When I was young, I would peek down the stairs when my parents had a party, which was often, and I recall feeling embarrassed that my mother was dancing so freely and with such pizzazz.

Rosalind and Nancy, 1944

As the years unfolded, Mom did learn to drive, but she was always home when we got in from high school, with a cup of tea waiting and an attentive ear to hear about our day. In my later teens, she gave me sound advice about boys and dating. The era of birth control pills had not yet arrived, and it was a dreaded fear of all parents that their daughter might get pregnant. Mom warned me in her gentle manner and caring calmness. She also imparted her strong opinions about women keeping their bank accounts in their own names and not going into debt. I never knew why she was so adamant about this.

She respected my getting on with my life. I still lived at home when I studied at university, as did my siblings. But I was focused on my future and my plans and was unaware of the mood in the house.

On a sunny day in June 1965, I had gone to church with my mother and sister. I was twenty-one, and my life was humming along. I had a serious boyfriend and was enjoying my first job after university. That afternoon the house erupted. My father was yelling and pounding on the locked master bedroom door, then racing down the street to find a neighbour who was a doctor. And then sirens sounded on the street, and firemen and police arrived.

In the chaos, I looked in the bedroom and saw my mother lying on her bed wearing her beautiful blue knit dress.

Oh my God, she was dead. What the hell happened? I couldn't take in the scene. I blocked my ears so I couldn't hear what was going on.

Trauma set in, and my memory of the events as they unfolded in those hours still remains jagged and disconnected.

Close family arrived. And quietly and quickly, a narrative was developed that she had died of a heart attack. I knew instinctively that wasn't true, but I couldn't fathom the word "suicide" either. My father hardly spoke at all.

The fateful day ended with a family friend coming by to give my siblings and me tranquilizers so we could sleep. Little blue pills! And we just took them without asking quite why.

The cover up with secrets and lies started to unfold in fast succession.

The minister visited the next day. A funeral was planned. My only two memories of it were odd snapshots from that day. I wore a favourite pale blue and pink coat with matching skirt. Strange that I didn't wear black. At our house after the funeral, as friends and family gathered, my mother's best friend, Marg, confronted me in the kitchen to ask me "What really happened?" She was insistent.

Knowing by then what to say, I blurted out the lie: Mom died of a heart attack. Then I turned quickly and fled upstairs.

My flashbacks of the next weeks and months are hazy, but one thing was certain in my mind: It was not a heart attack.

How can I make sense of this tragedy? I am not sure how to think. Suicide is a terrible blot on a family? A shame? Maybe not? What was my mother thinking? Why did she take her life? Why didn't she talk to me? To protect me and not bother me with her troubles? Did she tell anyone? Maybe Syl? But I can't ask her. No one is talking about the reality. There is a heavy code of silence being insisted on by everyone in the family. I need to know more! Who can I ask? Not my father. He is still not speaking. I am angry that I can't tell the truth. I have to perpetuate the coverup that she died of a heart attack. No, she didn't! It was suicide. Crazy making in my head!

For months, I dreamed that she was alive and just disappeared into another city. I tried in vain to find her, searching always for the elusive reassurance that she was coming home and all would be well again. The nightmare ended each time by waking to the truth, again and again. It never went away.

The secret of what really happened that day was locked in with the cover up that would not come to light, for years and years. From time to time, people would ask me about my mother and her death. I would feel so conflicted that I could not bring myself to tell the truth and just perpetuated the lie: She died of a heart attack.

And sometimes in my mind, I would try to rationalize that she died of a broken heart to make the lie not quite so blatant.

My brother believes she was depressed for years, but I never saw that. As I came to know a few months after my mother's death, my father was having an affair. My sister and I pieced together the secrets my father was guarding with random clues and whispers. My aunt Syl eventually told me that Mom knew and had tried to figure out how to leave the marriage. But she couldn't bring herself to do so because she was deeply aware of the stigma of a divorced woman in the 1960s.

How that fear led her to choose to leave the marriage by suicide at fifty-four remains for me the most tragic story of her life. If only she had talked to someone, if only she realized how much her death would affect us all forever. Her state of mind must have been so skewed to think that death was her only option. She must have been desperate.

It came to light later that Mom had changed her will three months before her death, leaving all her wealth to her three children and nothing to her husband. She had independent wealth from her family and had kept it separate as she had often advised me to do.

The year after my mother's death, I married my boyfriend. As I look back now, that too was a blur. But I needed to get out of the house and its memories and away from my father. My husband and I made a life together, buying a house, having three children, and living the quiet and calm existence of a typical 1960s and 1970s family. I stayed home, and my husband provided. I made the meals, sewed the girls' clothes, and gardened, much in the style of my mother twenty years earlier.

I was repeating the pattern of her life, but I was oblivious. I was playing a role just like she had—mother and daughter alike in so many ways. Like her, I plowed on.

I became involved in volunteer work, which gave me an outlet. But I knew that my duty, yes duty, was at home, making sure all was running smoothly. I believed that my needs came after those of my husband and my children. That was the model I grew up with.

After twenty years of marriage, when both my husband and I were in our early forties, our marriage had become stale and predictable. We had watched friends going through mid-life crises and commented how sad that was and how preventable. This wouldn't happen to us. So how did I not see how badly our marriage was crumbling?

With virtually no warning my husband announced he was having an affair with a neighbour and was leaving the marriage. Twenty years to the month that my mother had died!

As the mess of divorce unfolded—with fighting, legal battles, and therapy—I realized that in order for me to move forward in my life, the secret of my mother's death had to be unlocked. So I began to talk about her suicide, first with a therapist and then with friends. The lie was put to rest.

People were shocked. And I found out later that my husband's greatest fear about leaving our marriage was that I too would commit suicide. I knew I would never do that. I knew the devastation my mother's death had caused me and my siblings. I was not going to follow the pattern of her life anymore.

I forged ahead and found a career in the legal world and was extremely successful. I was sought after for volunteer jobs from a myriad of organizations and found deep satisfaction in these roles. I grew to understand that my life was now better and so much more fulfilling. I had much to offer the world, and I could put my needs first. I did have worth and value apart from being a mother.

And this new life was a positive example to my children, my daughters and my son, to aspire to. My children grew up and went their ways. There were bumps on the road with parenting, but all three have found meaningful careers, have chosen excellent life partners, and now have children of their own.

Maybe, I often ponder, I have taken on the traits of Rosalind, the Shakespearean heroine. I am independent minded, strong willed, good hearted, I think, and people say I am terribly clever. The trajectory of my life changed the pattern, and I survived and thrived for the next thirty-five years. I often think of my mother and wish so dearly that she could see me now. I know she would be proud of me and of my children. What she missed is overwhelmingly sad, but I will carry her legacy and hold her dear to me for all my days.

I will tell her story to anyone who will listen—not just the tragic part but the wonderful years of Rosalind's life too, when she was independent minded, strong willed, good hearted, and terribly clever.

No more secrets and lies.

Sylvia

The name comes from Shakespeare's *Two Gentlemen of Verona*, in which Sylvia is courageous, strong willed, and knows how to play life's game. Like Sylvia, my aunt was incredibly loyal and brave.

Sylvia was my aunt; my mother's older sister by four years. The first hint of her personality and interests could have been the letter she wrote to Santa Claus in 1914 at the age of seven. She asked for a toy gun and a soldier's suit. At the beginning of the First World War, it was much more likely something a boy would want.

Sylvia's older brother wasn't the son her father had hoped for. He was timid and awkward. So Sylvia, or Syl as she came to be known, took on the persona of the "son" in the family. By the time she was sixteen, she had a fascination with Annie Oakley and persuaded her parents to take her to the US for shooting lessons. She boasted about this adventure until the day she died.

Sylvia with her pipe, 1930s

As was the custom at the time and in the family in which she grew up, Syl was expected to be a young lady with cultural pursuits. She took up piano and became accomplished but never bothered to play once she had passed all her conservatory exams. She was more interested in outdoor adventures. One of her favourite activities in the summer was to shoot bullfrogs and then bring them home to have frog's legs for dinner.

And she loved to smoke a pipe.

Syl was expected to marry, but the one beau she had was called overseas at the beginning of the Second World War when she was thirty-two, and she chose to wait for him.

Henry was the love of her life, and they married, but not until 1946. By then she was almost forty, and sadly they had no children. But they did have a marvellous marriage with shared interests in hunting, adventure travelling, and drinking fine scotch.

Syl was so proud of her husband, who was a renowned and beloved doctor, as head of medicine at the Western Hospital. Most women of that era were known by their husband's name. But my aunt, who was not at all boastful, chose a subtle adaption: Mrs. Henry-Black, with a hyphen. It was a subtle variation, which pleased her.

She could fix anything and loved tinkering with tools and projects in her basement work room. She also was a meticulous seamstress and made many of her own clothes—mostly pant suits, not frilly dresses. Frugal was her mantra in all things.

Syl and her sister, my mother Roz, were fast friends and spent many hours together every week, whether running errands, sewing, or having tea. They were vastly different in many ways. Syl was the tomboy who preferred plain clothes and sometimes a tie or vest. Roz was the epitome of fashion and elegance with a feminine persona. They did share common interests in theatre, music, gardening, and sewing, and they had each other's backs in all matters.

As I grew up, Syl was an integral part of our family. Christmas would not be Christmas without Syl and Henry arriving for breakfast in the morning. She was the family chronicler of photographs and memorabilia, which I appreciate so much more now than I did then.

Her life took a tragic turn when she was fifty-seven. Henry died suddenly of a massive heart attack. Losing the love of her life was so devastating that she wasn't even able to attend his funeral because she was so grief stricken. Roz was an enormous support that year. But then a year later, as if life had not handed out enough bad cards, Roz took her own life. Syl had now lost the two most important people in her world. She was bereft and completely shattered.

But then, rising from these dual tragedies, a new role appeared for her as our surrogate mother. My sister, brother, and I were in total shock at our mother's untimely death, and our aunt needed a new focus. She became our rock, our shoulder, our anchor. She was always available to be with us, to help us and to give us guidance, and always without being intrusive. Maybe because she wasn't my mother, I took to her advice with more acceptance. But she was truly gifted in knowing how and when to help. And she absolutely knew how to listen.

So a new chapter started with Syl as a central part of my life. She was generous with her time as I married, had three children, and got on with my life. She babysat, brought cookies, repaired clothes, gardened, and made the most delicious meals for us.

She specialized in old-style foods, chicken à la king, Finnan Haddie, potato latkes, and cheese scones. And she was an expert at preserving mustard pickle, jams, jellies, and such.

Not one to be idle, Syl kept on with her sewing, grew an amazing flower and vegetable garden, and continued to find time for projects in her work room. And she travelled far and wide. I always was amazed that she could go on a three-week trip and pack only the smallest carry-on suitcase. She would say she didn't need much. What was in that bag was always a mystery.

When I was in my forties and dealing with my marriage ending, there was no more welcoming sanctuary than her home. A glass of wine, a home cooked meal, and an ear to listen were a tonic for my broken heart.

Sadly though, I couldn't talk over the facts of my mother's suicide. It just wasn't a subject she could deal with. I am not even sure how I knew this, but we had a tacit agreement not to go there. The family secrecy lasted with her. She was resentful and angry at my father and, I guess, blamed him for my mother's death, but she never spoke of that either. It was another road that we didn't travel down.

Syl continued her hunting pursuits, now using a sling shot to scare away the marauding raccoons that were getting into her vegetables. Her diligence and detail in preserving the family stories were a labour of love for her. She made scrapbooks for me and my siblings of my mother's dance career, with photos and newspaper clippings she had saved. She wrote details of her parents and their lives. She put photos in little albums with notes and dates of all the relatives. These treasured memories have kept me connected to the past in so many ways and warmed my heart and soul when I wondered again and again about my mother and her life.

In her eighties, my aunt started helping at a school library repairing books. They loved her at the school, and she was happy to still have usefulness. I think that was her middle name.

And she had her dogs, always miniature schnauzers, one after the other, all named either Percy or Pepys. She was a fixture in her neighbourhood walking the dog, with her deer stalker hat and down coat, and of course her pant suit.

Rarely did Syl don a dress. The one occasion was the annual Henry Black dinner to give a fellowship award for a medical expert to come to speak at the hospital. She fussed and worried about that evening all year. Clearly her love of Henry and her pride at being Mrs. Henry-Black never faded.

As she aged, Syl fretted about many things in her past, all of which she kept tightly bottled up. My mother's death and her inability to talk of it were likely top of mind. On my suggestion, in her eighties, she started visiting a psychotherapist to unburden her anxieties. She never spoke of what was on her mind but always said she felt better for seeing her therapist. She continued until the year before she died at ninety-two.

Generous of spirit, interesting and interested, she lives on in my memory, not just as a favourite aunt but as an amazing woman, who was, in so many ways, ahead of her time. She was her own person through and through. Loyal and brave. My life was so much richer having her as my second mother—a shoulder to lean on and an anchor to ground me.

How lucky was I to have been in her orbit for so many years.

2. Jennifer Walcott

Jennifer Walcott is a retired teacher of English living in Toronto. She started writing poetry as a child in Jamaica and has maintained her love of writing since then. She draws inspiration and courage to write from her generous writing partners, former students, and family. She has had her verses published in *Calling Cards: New Poetry from Caribbean/Canadian Women, Your Daily Poem.com, Calabash*, and *The Antigonish Review*.

Hyacinth

My Mother's Hands

A memory, perhaps, propels
my mother's hands,
or maybe they move
just to show they're still alive.
They are travellers,
an unceasing
back and forth,
bone and blotchy skin
over and over
her purse,
her lap,
the chair,
my back.

She was a soft-spoken gentle woman with a cast-iron core.

She'd drop her voice to say, "I was illegitimate" or to ask her daughters, "Are you pregnant?" She never swore or used coarse language. And even when she was severely hard of hearing, she'd smile politely and try to answer the questions she thought she'd been asked. She lived frugally, surviving on her old age security income while still donating to many charities, ten and twenty dollars at a time. From those limited resources, she was able to spread her love over her family. When she travelled to visit her daughter and grandchildren in St. Louis, she took biscuits, notepads, t-shirts and sweaters, as well as bits and bobs, mostly useless but always appreciated. "Here comes Grandma with a suitcase full of love," granddaughter Michele once observed. Her politics were always left of centre, and she'd vote for democratic socialists unless it was for Trudeau. She adored Pierre, cried when he died, and collected every commemorative magazine she could find. She loved to talk politics when she could bemoan corruption, small mindedness, and greed. The Harris years in Ontario provided lots of fodder for conversations that usually began with "I don't know how the poor people will manage." My friends all loved her for her sweetness and generosity—the baby clothes she knitted as well as the t-shirts she brought back from visits to Jamaica. Sometimes she'd forget a child's age, as with Nathan, whom she forever thought of as a five-year-old, even when he was a lanky teenager.

And the cast-iron core? Was that just for her daughters?

She and I fought often about silly mother-daughter things. She was heavy handed, literally, as she slapped me and threw things. I remember being boxed on Oxford Street in London as well as having a hairbrush broken on my ankle and a high-heeled shoe thrown with such precision that it hit my coccyx and

I couldn't sit without pain for weeks.

She once emptied my closet and put everything on my bed because she had gone in there and found a shoe brush on a shelf where it obviously didn't belong. I was angry and bundled everything in the bedspread and dumped it in her room. She looked at me for a few seconds, then calmly kicked everything out the front door onto the verandah.

I remember trying to sit in her lap as a small child, maybe five or so years old, and being pushed off. I wanted to nuzzle her, but she didn't like that. I don't remember ever being hugged or cuddled and she certainly never said that she loved me. In fact, my two sisters and I confronted her about that once when we were all adults. We ganged up on her in a bathroom and insisted that she say, "I love you" before we'd let her out. Belinda used to force her to say it as well. If a grandchild said, "I love you, Grandma," she'd reply, "Me too." Belinda insisted she say, "I love you."

But her iron was of another kind.

This is the woman who divorced an adulterous, abusive husband in 1952 or 53 and then returned to work in nursing while scattering her daughters to boarding school and relatives. This is the woman who moved her family from Jamaica to England in 1960 and took work as a housekeeper, something far below her station and ability, because she wanted to give the unmarried daughter who'd had a child a fresh start. This is the woman who uprooted herself again in 1962 to return to Jamaica because I, the youngest, was being sidelined in school because of race, and she was not going to allow that. This is the woman who let me go to my neglectful father in 1966, hoping this time he'd keep his word and give me an education in Canada. He didn't. She and my aunt did.

I was a single parent most of my daughter's early life, so I know how hard it is. My mother did it for three girls, and she never complained; she just straightened her back and got on with it. Her life was not one of abundance or ease; she made do and never appeared to ask for more. Her sister Carmen, whom she admired, probably helped her the most, but if so, it was done quietly.

She was not one to blame or to wallow in self-pity. In fact, she often told me that if I recognized some hurt, I should fix it or just get over it. Nor was she one to praise. She taught me that I should always work to the best of my ability and that the reward was in knowing I'd done a good job. Once, and once only, I overheard her say to someone that she was proud of the work I was doing in Jamaica, following in Carmen's footsteps.

Hyacinth and Jennifer, 2002

Her mantra was the AA affirmation: "God grant me the serenity to accept the things I cannot change, the courage to change the things I can, and the wisdom to know the difference." She also loved the line from "Invictus": "I am the master of my fate. I am the captain of my soul."

So, although she had a cast-iron core of self-sufficiency and self-reliance, as well as an accompanying inability to show tenderness or vulnerability, she also demonstrated love through acts of kindness and gift-giving.

My mother's name was Hyacinth, and like the flower, she was beautiful and exuded a strong presence. But I also find the flower a bit cloying, and I see how that element mirrors the parts of my mother that I find difficult. I no longer blame her because I know she did the best she could and that life had dealt her some serious blows.

Her conception, birth, and early childhood were shrouded in shame and neglect, so that core was developed out of self-preservation. She gave everything she had to us, but I see the resulting deficiency in myself: my emotional underdevelopment, my harshness, my scorn of abundance, my impatience with needy people, and my reluctance to praise. Maybe I should just take her advice and fix it or get over it.

Advice

Do you know, little girl,
what can happen,
how this lap can close
like a bank vault,
lock you out
force you to stand up
for yourself?

Yet she deserves so much more from me because I, of her three daughters, spent the most time with her, and I am the most like her, I think.

My first memories of her are of visiting her at the YWCA hostel on North Street in Kingston. The building was a huge, gorgeous colonial structure with dark mahogany floors, high ceilings, rooms running every which way off corridors, and gingerbread trim on all the verandahs.

Aunt Carmen, who was in charge, had the best room on the top floor and that was where we children always played because she had a shelf of books for all of the nieces and nephews, and we were allowed to read them at our leisure.

Hyacinth's room was further away, and I only remember an ashtray made of pennies and all her beaded necklaces that I put on to play dress-up. There were many other women living there and some of them let me play in their rooms when I visited.

I don't know when, but Hyacinth soon moved from the YWCA up to the university hospital, where she was the home sister with a stiff white uniform, a red belt, and a nurse's cap. My sisters took me to visit her there, where she had a room with a small bed, a table, and lots of books.

She also had a sewing machine, I know, because she made me dresses. One I remember was a blue and white striped material, and she sewed on an appliqué pocket that looked like a flower in a flowerpot. I loved that dress. One of her books was about nursing, and it had cartoon drawings, which I looked at and about which I made up my own stories. She also had a blender and made me milkshakes with Horlicks and vanilla ice cream.

My sisters and I were living with our father at this time, and the two separate worlds were not strange to me at all, as that was all I knew.

In April 1960, we moved to England, and I lived with my mother for the first time since I was a baby. This was where our battles began, as she tried to discipline me, and I resisted. My sisters are ten and twelve years older than I, but I fancied myself their age so was probably incredibly mouthy and difficult. I remember learning that famous four-letter word and using it all the time for effect. Hyacinth made me write it out five hundred times one Saturday morning, and when I was done, I wrote her a note: "I hope you're fucking satisfied."

Whenever I was punished for some transgression, I would demand she show me my adoption papers because I could not be her child and be treated so unfairly. I would write long letters of complaint to my father, who lived in Canada, asking him to rescue me from this tyrant. I hope with all my heart she did not mail them.

Yes, I was a challenging child, wilful and rude. Was this my defence against insecurity? By the time I was nine years old, I had lived with my parents, then with an aunt and uncle, then with my father, then with my grandmother and aunt, and then with my mother. The flat in England was the seventh house I'd lived in. Every place was different, with different rules. But the common feature was that a child was supposed to be seen and not heard. I had that maxim levelled at me many times. But I was determined to be seen and heard.

Hyacinth remained calm. She'd hit me or throw things in frustration, but she did not yell, nor was she moody or angry. She sighed a lot. She also created what I now see as a circle of support around me. The family she worked for was well connected, and I was included in outings with their children. I remember going to Devon for a holiday and having lunches with interesting people in homes all over London. I remember a party in which some British movie stars attended and having a session with one of Hyacinth's employers, who were both psychiatrists.

When I announced that I no longer believed in god, a Caribbean family friend and his wife came to lunch. I was left alone with Rev. Philip Potter after lunch to have a chat about my stance. To his credit, we agreed to disagree. But he and his wife had me visit them on several occasions when they took me to concerts and galleries and even had me perform in a fundraising concert with Methodist children at the Royal Albert Hall. Rev. Potter later became the head of the World Council of Churches and was always a family friend, but he never again questioned my lack of faith. In fact, although the family remained Christian and quite devout, no one ever bothered me about my agnosticism.

We moved back to Jamaica because the school I attended in Muswell Hill said I had failed the 11Plus exams and should attend a secondary modern trade school, not a grammar school, which was the academic stream. Given my loathing of standardized tests, I probably did fail the exam, but my academic ability was not in question.

So Hyacinth arranged for me to go to St. Andrew High School in Jamaica and to sit the Jamaican common entrance exams later in the year. These I passed, and my four years at "Andrews" were pivotal in creating character, friendships, and a love of learning. I recall now how she encouraged my friendships, allowed boys to visit me at home, let me go to parties, let me visit older cousins and their families who lived nearby, and arranged for a math tutor for me. She also defended me against the grandmother who lived with us and who, in her dementia, accused me of all sorts of lies and thefts.

We had no television in Jamaica, but some weekend evenings, Hyacinth would make popcorn and mix a shandy—beer and ginger ale—and we'd share these while we read. Those four years back in Jamaica might have been easier as I grew into adolescence, but some of that old resistance lingered. It was during these years that she put all my clothes out on the verandah. And it was during these years that she told me how she had defied my father's wish that she abort me.

Perhaps to prove how much she loved and wanted me, one evening she told me that my father had arranged for her to have an abortion when she was pregnant. This was ten years after my older sister was born, after many years of estrangement, as my father already had his other woman, who became his second wife. Why he came to her bed she never knew, but he was definite about not wanting a third child; he was on his way out the door after all. She agreed, but then she reneged, and here I am.

They divorced shortly after I was born, I suppose, as I have no memory of living with them. Her brother and his wife had a daughter who was a few months younger and a second daughter, who was just born, so I went to live with them. That home is the first I remember, and not fondly, but that is another tale.

My father had my sisters and me with him for perhaps a year before he took off to Canada. Arthur was handsome and charming and feckless. His mother adored him and allowed him to think he was entitled to the adoration of others. Hyacinth might have provided that for a while. The only photograph of them is of two incredibly handsome young people, their heads together, smiling sweetly at the camera.

He visited Jamaica when I was fifteen, and it was the first time I'd seen him in ten years. He had this grand idea that I should come to Canada and live with him and his wife and son, and he'd make sure I went to university. Why did Hyacinth agree to this? It fits with her efforts on behalf of her daughters, always doing what she thought would afford us more opportunities, a better chance in life.

But she knew Arthur to be a liar. The night he came to our home to discuss this plan with her was the first time I remember seeing them in the same room together, and it made me feel scared and sick. I left the house and went to one of my cousins across the street. Yet the idea of going to Canada filled me with excitement, and it was a good decision, despite the hurt and frustration it created.

In 1979, Hyacinth came to Canada to live with me and my first husband, who generously offered to sponsor her. Hyacinth was always grateful to David for this chance, and he appears to have positive memories of her as well. For the next five years, I had the chance to see her differently because she was the primary caregiver for our daughter.

I have only just worked out that Hyacinth was the age I am now when she was looking after Rachael. She seemed older to me then than I do to myself now, but that is true of us all, I suspect. What I do share with her is the complete joy that being a grandmother creates. She was wonderful as Grandma. Of course, she sewed clothes and knitted blankets and sweaters, made milk puddings and porridge, and took her turn walking and rocking the baby to sleep at night. She also showed Rachael how to properly use the record player so she could play our Sharon, Lois, & Bram record, and she gave her a straight pin and a piece of cloth so she could sew alongside Grandma.

She would bring Rachael to the bus stop to meet me when I came home from work and take her to the shops and to the park. What I saw as she cared for my daughter was her loving patience—qualities I did not feel as a child, but which I now recognize were always there, just not in ways I could see or hear.

I live in a world of words; I need to talk or write to understand myself, whereas Hyacinth lived in a world of thoughts and small actions. She felt she didn't need to tell her children that she loved us because she felt love and that love guided her actions. That love made her sacrifice all she did for her daughters, and she never felt the need to explain those choices to us; we were just expected to know that she was acting in our best interests.

I think now of all the things she did for me along with raising Rachael until she was six years old. She would show up at my apartment with some gadget for the kitchen that I didn't even realize I needed. She bought me a washer and dryer when she saw how hard it was for me to go to the laundromat each week. She held me and remained silent when a particularly destructive love affair ended. She was there with her soft voice and cast-iron core when I needed her, and I see now just how much I gained from her. Is it possible to love someone more after they have died?

Seeking Forgiveness

For most of my life, I have carried a deep resentment and anger towards my middle sister, Mary. She was named after my mother's mother, the grandmother we never knew because she was sent away to Panama in 1914, when she became pregnant with her brother-in-law's child. That child, my mother Hyacinth, was born in Panama and then sent back to Jamaica to her father's family when she was eight years old. Hyacinth carried a sense of shame about her illegitimacy all her life, and I think she imbued me with a sense that pregnancy outside of marriage was a terrible sin.

When I was a child of seven, Mary had a child. It was a secret, and I was admonished for speaking about it. Middle-class girls should not get themselves in trouble. That child was quickly adopted, and then our mother took us all to England for a fresh start.

But Mary did not start over; she decided to repeat her actions and was pregnant a second time. For most of my life, I wondered what happened to that second child she had in England. As a teenager and adult, I would try to talk to Mary about the two children she had and gave away. Did she know where they were? Did she want to get in touch? She would shut me down immediately and refused to talk about them.

That reaction surprised and irritated me for a long time. I was angry with her for years because I saw her as irresponsible and selfish. How dare she pretend not to have children? Recently, though, I have been working on seeing her reaction in a different light. She might have felt such guilt that her only way to cope was to suppress and avoid.

I see now that Mary used avoidance in many areas of her life. Take, for example, how she ran her event planning business. She refused to create a website and dealt with contracts orally; she would not hire anyone to whom she could entrust tasks, working mainly with her friends or people to whom she could assign simple tasks that she'd then micromanage.

Did she have a learning disability? She never pursued any training after leaving school as soon as she could. How much brain damage had she sustained after her stroke in the mid-eighties? Mary relied on her considerable charm and huge social circle to survive. Her business was small, dependent on a few loyal annual contracts. She was foolish about money and never saved or invested, so ended her life virtually broke, relying on friends and rationing her medication.

Her health was precarious. She was diagnosed with lupus at one time. She had cITP, a low platelet count; she had type 2 diabetes, a stroke, a heart attack, cataracts, and rheumatoid arthritis. She took so many pills that I wondered how she could keep them straight and often reminded her to write them down.

Mary was always well known and popular because she could be fun and kind, and up until her stroke, she was a beauty. After the stroke, she was prescribed steroids and gained a lot of weight. She was often short of breath and in pain, so she stopped any form of exercise. Her many friends were always generous and kind to her, as she was to them.

She showed her family a different side. With me, the inquisitive younger sister, and my daughter, she was critical and sharp tongued. She was like this also with one of our nieces, who was a single mother, as was I. Was she jealous that we were able to keep our children and provide for them?

She took money from our eldest sister and never paid it back. Although Mary was the main caregiver for our Aunt Carmen and our mother Hyacinth in their last years, she often expressed irritation with her role, never mind that these women gave her a place to live and contributed financially to their own upkeep. She sold off many of our aunt's fine paintings and antique furniture to pay her debts. My eldest sister, her daughters, my daughter, and I all found Mary irritating and grating. To me, she was loud and self-centered and demanding.

I always wondered about her children; more than curiosity, it was almost as if there was some duty that I owed them. I have no information that could help me trace the first child, but after Mary died, I spoke with a couple of people who knew her in England and who could at least tell me that she took the second child to Scotland to be adopted before she returned to Jamaica in 1964. I thought about using an adoption tracing company to find this child, but I didn't have enough information.

Then, recently, I agreed to DNA testing at the urging of a friend interested in genealogy. I had no expectations of finding Mary's children and agreed to the test more to find out my ethnic background. The test provided me with a link to Mary's child and grandchild and to information that filled in some of the gaps.

Everything I have learned about the child Mary had, and left, stoked my old anger and resentment toward her. This child's life has not been easy, and no contact with me is desired; a fact I accept, sadly. But Mary is now dead and knows nothing of what I have learned, cannot answer questions, or even atone for her actions. What then am I left with?

How much of her illnesses were due to suppressed guilt and remorse? I see them as metaphors. Bad blood. Weak heart. Heart failure as cause of death. Writing this is forcing me to try to understand her, and that is helping me to release the anger and resentment I have felt towards her for most of my life. Forgiveness is what I believe I want, for her and for myself. Maybe soon I will be able to say, "poor Mary."

I have found Mary's child and grandchild. I know their names. I have seen photographs of them. Their stories are not mine to tell. And even though I still have some questions, I no longer feel driven by curiosity, nor do I feel angry. Instead, I feel that I can try to forgive Mary because I am trying to understand her. Seeking forgiveness is a new feeling, a better one.

The Two Marys

Grandma Mary slipped,
or was pushed,
then sent away
to hide the shame.

She bore the child
and named as father
the steadfast man
she later married.
She bore more children,
loved them with a gentle hand.

But that first, our mother,
was sent back
into her father's fold
where no amount of love
could overcome the shame
she felt about her
unplanned birth.

When sister Mary rushed
to repeat this history,
Mother's inbred shame
rushed out to meet it.
She took us all away
from Mary's first mistake.

But sister Mary lapsed.
She bore a second child.
Named the real father
but lied about her name.
Left the child with a promise
she never would fulfill.

With her no loving gentleness
just harsh avoidance,
a cold-seeming heart
shaped by inherited shame.

3. Melanie Faye

Melanie Faye—mother, grandmother, and retired psychotherapist—was born and educated in apartheid South Africa. She emigrated to Canada to give her children a better life untainted by racism. Her retirement project is to compile a family history, a legacy for her children and grandchildren. Never having written anything other than academic papers, she joined the memoir writing workshop at the Academy for Lifelong Learning Toronto, where she found support and encouragement. It was in a small group of spirited and talented women writers that she found the courage to write. Her love of myths, gods and goddesses, fairy tales, and the psychology of self and spirit is reflected in her writing. She can be found in the kitchen still making chicken and matzoh ball soup for her children and grandchildren.

Snake: A Dream

In 1877, Friedrich Nietzsche wrote, "The snake that cannot shed its skin has to die. As well the minds which are prevented from changing their opinions; they cease to be minds."

I had a dream, not a Martin Luther King kind of a dream, but a sleep dream, one that put me on a path I might otherwise not have taken.

Since time immemorial, snakes have shown up in the mythologies of many peoples worldwide, and they showed up in my dream—two pythons came to visit. They were huge, magnificent creatures; one sat on each of my shoulders, whispering something in my ears. I was excited and delighted they were there. I felt I was being given a gift. The feeling tone in the dream was one of joy. I felt excited, energized, passionate, fully alive, and curious.

Perhaps these feelings make no sense. Are these not two extremely dangerous and deadly creatures that could crush me to death? Should I have not been very, very afraid? Perhaps, but I was not. I was elated.

I have had dreams that did terrify me. Dreams from which I woke up with my heart pounding, out of breath and cold with sweat. Nightmares I can still recall, even some from childhood. There were other dreams that elicited deep and intense feelings: feelings of betrayal, sadness, pain, hope, despair, and some that lingered long after waking. I know the intensity of dream feelings, and my pythons brought with them not terror, but excitement and curiosity. What were they trying to tell me? What gift did they have for me?

At the time of this dream, I was training to be a psychotherapist. Dream interpretation was part of that training. I could hardly wait to take this dream into a group session for interpretation. I had great respect for the group therapist and was in awe of him.

Then, to my surprise, I was crushed by his interpretation. I cannot recall exactly what he said, but it was biblical. He seemed shocked that I had positive feelings about this dream. These creatures were not my friends. Did I not know I should be afraid, very afraid? I do remember him saying something about believing my own delusions.

What I heard might not have been exactly what he said, but the Biblical Judeo-Christian interpretation of the snake was insinuated—the tempter of evil deeds, self-deception, falling from grace, being denigrated as the perpetrator of deceit, the shame of being a woman, to be expelled from the Garden, and thus to suffer the consequences of bad decisions and ungodly choices. I might not have heard his exact words, but I surely understood their underlying meaning.

I have always believed and trusted my dream feelings. So why not now?

The therapist was a Jungian analyst, trained at the Jungian Institute in Geneva. I had absolute trust and faith in his interpretation of symbols. I took what he said to heart and came away feeling deflated, embarrassed, foolish, and self-critical, judging myself as stupid. I am familiar with the biblical story, so how could I have missed the overtly obvious symbolism and believe I could be a psychotherapist? I chastised myself severely and came away despondent, depressed, and depleted of energy and enthusiasm. Worse than that, I was shamed and ashamed, and my confidence was shattered.

For weeks, maybe even months, my snake dream niggled at me, tugged at me, and demanded I pay attention to it. It would not go away or leave me in peace. Then I began to explore the ancient snake myths, and a whole exciting world opened up for me. A world that led to the exploration of myth, astrology, and fairy tales. A world full of mystery, magic, exotic stories, symbolism, and meaning.

I have been exploring that world with great joy and enthusiasm ever since—a world in which the snake is a symbol of transformation, shedding the past, letting go of the old and embracing the new, where the snake is the goddess of feminine wisdom.

In many cultures, past and present, the snake is given a positive interpretation as a symbol of transformation and rebirth. In India, even the deadly cobra is a sacred animal. In the biblical story, the snake, the serpent, brought sin, not transformation, into the world—a woman being the one who tempted man to sin. The woman as sinner does not appear in other religions, mythologies, or creation stories. The biblical snake is the only one that is negatively interpreted.

What I failed to realize at the time was that the therapist, while well trained at the famous and highly regarded Jung Institute, was also deeply steeped in Catholicism. He could not shed his biblical and patriarchal symbolism of the snake. I had trusted an outside authority rather than what I intuitively knew.

The pythons gave me two gifts: my power restored and the return of imagination. I was inspired to revisit and recover the magical, fantastical, fairy tale time of my childhood, and in the process to shed past anger and pain.

Eden: A South African Childhood

The South African garden of my childhood was a magical place for me. I spent hours watching garden snails glide across the ground leaving silvery trails behind them. They were actually a menace in the garden. It seems they had voracious appetites and, small though they were, they wreaked destruction among the plants. I watched with cruel fascination when the gardener poured salt on them. The salt caused their delicate bodies to bubble and froth, killing them.

There were all sorts of creepy crawlies and flying insects in the garden. We called them miggies and ghoghas (pronounced with a guttural sound at the back of the throat). Miggies flew, and ghoghas crawled. Both words have their origins in Afrikaans, although ghogha may well be derived from khoikahoi, a word from the San language. It is also used as a term of endearment spoken to small children.

There were red-and-black spotted lady bugs and stink bugs, which gave off a foul smell if you crushed them, and beetles of all shapes and sizes. When flipped onto their backs, beetles frantically kick their legs in an attempt to right themselves. Unless some kind child comes along and flips them right side up, they will die.

The privet hedge, which ran the length of the garden from the street to the backyard, housed all kinds of caterpillars, from small pale green ones to brightly coloured and patterned ones that could get as big as a large adult thumb. I would get lost watching the up and down motion of their bodies as they lurched their way forwards. They sting, and it is painful, so I had to be careful not to touch them. I learned from experience what I could touch and what I should not touch.

My favourite of all these small creatures was the shongololo, a millipede. The name is derived from the Xhosa and Zulu word "ubushonga," meaning to roll up, which is what the shongololo does to protect its soft underparts. They live hidden in cracks and crevices and come out after a rain. I spent many happy moments watching them march around in search of decaying plant matter. When disturbed, they escape by moving away in a slithering snakelike motion intended to scare away predators. They did not scare me. It was easy to stop them from getting away just by touching them. They would curl up in a ball and play dead.

My garden was populated by a variety of small and wondrous creatures, including fairies—my secret playmates—who lived at the bottom of the front garden. They never went to the back yard; it was too busy there.

On a day long, long ago, a day that is still with me in memory and feeling, I was skipping up the garden path with my fairy pals when I spotted my mother peeking at me from behind the living room curtains. I cannot explain what happened next. I felt spied upon; my closely guarded and cherished secret had been exposed, and the fairies vanished, never to return. I was four or five years old when the magic left the garden. I forgot about the fairies and the magic and went about the business of growing up, going to school, and learning to read and write and ride a bike, doing whatever five-year-olds did.

Even so, our backyard was a child's paradise, a veritable Eden. This was where mud pies were made; ripe fruits were plucked from trees—peaches, plums, granadillas, nectarines, figs, and pomegranates. This was where we played hide and seek, cops and robbers, as well as cowboys and Indians. This was where large Black women scooped me up into their arms, protected me, fed me, and allowed me to run a little feral.

In this Eden, there was a crop of tall, sturdy bamboo that reached up to the garage roof. Like Tarzan, we held onto a stalk and swung off the garage roof. Pure joy! This was where nobody panicked if I took a tumble or scraped a knee, where I was not stifled or restricted by the rules of society's niceties. This was happiness.

One of the greatest delights of my childhood was eating outside with our servants, sitting on the thick, lush kikuyu grass under the peach tree in the backyard. The meal was always the same, beef stew and putupap, a firm cornmeal concoction somewhat like a firm, sticky polenta. With your fingers, you took some pap from the communal pot and used it to scoop up some beef stew from another communal pot and then popped it into your mouth. I was taught to be sure to never allow my fingers to touch my mouth, not even my lips.

As young children, we were left under the watchful eyes of our nannies to explore our immediate world of backyards. In Black South African culture, your mother's sisters were also your mothers. Perhaps it followed that your neighbour's nanny was also your nanny and would look out for wandering children.

My mother was out a lot, leaving my sister and me in the care of the nanny.

As an older child, my favourite book was *Grimm's Fairy Tales*. Many of the tales were dark and scary. I still have my original, complete, and illustrated edition depicting fire-breathing dragons, ugly, deformed goblins, devils with great horns, and snarling beasts with huge teeth that could devour you in one bite. There were tales of great adventures in shadowy realms; there were kings and queens, villains, as well as heroes and heroines, who sometimes died but were brought back to life by supernatural means; there was the breaking of evil spells and helpful animals with special powers. These were magical tales that both scared and thrilled me. They were my initiation into that magical, fantastical world that my snake dream brought back to me.

At some point in my childhood, there came a dawning of understanding that the people in whose care I was left were not respected and were looked on with disdain.

My happiness was marred by racism towards the very people entrusted to care for me—who were considered third-class citizens. My sister and I were left for hours on end to be cared for by people who were not my equals and thought to be incompetent, lazy, and ungrateful. But these were the people I had grown attached to. They were loving and kind and took good care of me. What is a child supposed to make of this?

Racism: My Country's, My Mother's, and My Own

*To think of man in terms of white, black or yellow is more
than an error. It is an eye disease, a cancer of the soul.*

—Rabbi Abraham Joshua Heschel,
Conference on Religion and Race,
January 14, 1963

I was born white in South Africa, where racial segregation had existed long
before I was born. I drank racism in with my mother's milk.

When the Nationalist Party came into power in 1948, apartheid (Afrikaans for "apartness") was legislated into law by an all-white government, and
policies of racial segregation were enforced. I was raised and came of age in
apartheid South Africa under a white supremacist government with fascist
and Nazi leanings.

Everywhere there were signs saying "whites only"—whites-only park
benches, whites-only drinking fountains, whites-only buses, whites-only public
toilets, whites-only playgrounds, and whites-only entrances to banks, the post
office, and other buildings.

My mother was a kind-hearted, warm, caring, and gentle person and
generous to a fault. Her heart genuinely ached for the plight of the Black
African community. In her own small, local way, she did what she could to
alleviate the pain and suffering of the Black people in her orbit. Yet she was
also racist.

If she were alive, she would be affronted and deeply hurt by being called
racist. Her experience with anti-Semitism and persecution—her family had
fled the pogroms in Russia— had made her compassionate and sympathetic to
the Black community. However, being deeply steeped in the racist milieu of
the day, where racist attitudes were normalized, she was oblivious to her own
racism.

Growing up, it was confusing to understand my mother's genuine concern
for Black people on the one hand and her blatant racism on the other. She
voiced all kinds of racial slurs: They were stupid, incompetent, lazy, and
unreliable. I knew from the click of her tongue and the shake of her head,
before she even spoke, that she considered that something one servant or
another had done was stupid.

I knew from a very young age that the people who bathed me, fed me, took
care of me, and were not allowed to use my toilet were beneath me. Even as a
child, I also made unreasonable demands, gave orders, shouted at the servants,
and generally expected them to do my bidding. I cringe as memories of my
past behaviour creep into consciousness even as I try to push them down.

Every White South African householder, including my mother, would tell you
how good they were to their servants. It usually meant they paid their servants

more than the going wage. This was said with pride, despite the fact that higher than the prevailing wages was still not sufficient to live on with dignity.

When I was growing up in the 1950s, we had no Black friends or acquaintances; the only Black people in our orbit were servants. We had three live-in servants: two women both named Emily—"Thin Emily" the nanny and "Fat Emily" the cook—and a houseboy called Johannes. This "boy" was a grown man and considerably older than his boss, my mother.

Our servants were not given the dignity of being identified by their own last names. When I visited a friend in South Africa in 1996, her daughter-in-law was musing about, and bemused by, the fact that she and my friends both had maids with the same name, Janey. And both maids were called Janey Fletcher, Fletcher being my friend's and her daughter-in-law's family name. I was taken aback that this practice of giving your servants your family name still persisted late into the twentieth century, suggesting ownership and harkening back to the time of slavery.

Our servants' quarters, with their monastic, cell-like rooms, were hidden from view behind a high, vine-covered trellis; in the spring, it displayed purple and white granadilla (passion fruit) flowers, and in autumn, it was laden with purple-black fruit. The brick building, with its cold concrete floors, was forbidden to us. We disobeyed, of course. My nanny's room smelled faintly sweet—a sweetness tinged with the smell of camphor and Vicks VapoRub. Camphor was said to ward off polio.

All three servants had their beds on bricks, high off the floor. The prevailing myth was that this prevented the Tokoloshe, a small and malevolent evil spirit, from reaching the bed and taking your life. The myth came about through Indigenous South African folklore to explain why people inexplicably died while sleeping in their rondavels (round huts). It was traditional to sleep on the floor on grass mats encircling a wood fire. Those who happened to sleep in an elevated position escaped the deadly curse of the Tokoloshe.

On one of the visits to my nanny's room—I was about ten—I asked about the Tokoloshe and the raised beds. She laughed and said the raised beds were because the floor was cold, and the room so small that she needed space under the bed to store her possessions. I briefly wondered why my mother did not give them a carpet and a wardrobe. And then I went out to play without giving it another thought.

It has always been a source of wonder to me that our servants—despite being put down, disparaged, and looked upon as inferior beings—were so warm, loving, kind, caring, and gentle with the children of their white oppressors.

Just as the proslavery Southerners in America turned the biblical curse of Ham (Genesis 9:2I-27) into justification for slavery and used it as God's reason for condemning generations of dark-skinned people from Africa to slavery, so did the Apartheid government use it to justify their oppression of Black people in South Africa. Most of those in power regarded themselves as good Christians and insisted that the rationalization for apartheid was right there in the Bible.

In Genesis (9:20-27), we are told that Noah had three sons: Shem, Ham, and Japheth. One day, they came across Noah lying drunk and naked in his tent. Shem and Japheth covered their father and did not look upon Noah's nakedness. When Noah awoke, knowing and ashamed that Ham had seen his nakedness, he cursed Ham's son, Canaan. Noah said, "Blessed be the Lord, the God of Shem and let Canaan be his servant. May God enlarge Japheth, and let him dwell in the tents of Shem, and let Canaan be his servant."

Nowhere in this account were Noah and his family described in racial terms, but as the story came down through the centuries, Ham and his descendants came to be portrayed as Black. They were condemned to servitude, and thus the idea of racial hierarchy was codified. This curse became the foundational text for apartheid.

All around me, people made racist comments. Black people were uncouth and uncivilized. They spoke so loudly you could hear them a mile away. It was true—they did speak loudly—but it was part of the Black South African culture to do so in order that people around you know you are not telling secrets or gossiping. My mother and most of the whites had no interest in getting to know or understand African culture.

While the powerful white South African minority, who were outnumbered ten to one, looked to the Bible for their guiding philosophy, the Bantu ethnic group, who were disparaged under apartheid rule, lived by a different philosophy: ubuntu.

Ubuntu was either unknown or of little interest to the white minority. It is an African concept meaning "humanity towards others." Our humanity is affirmed when we reach out and positively touch another's life. It is society, not a transcendent being, that gives humans their humanity. I am because you are.

The principles of ubuntu philosophy are respect, empathy, dignity, sharing, and compassion. Ubuntu promotes collective responsibility. Through our warmth, generosity, mutual support, and the sharing of skills, all can prosper.

How do you harden your heart against a people with such a fine life philosophy?

Nonetheless, I succumbed to the cultural expectations and norms of my generation. I married young, bought the house with the proverbial white picket fence, had servants, and left my children with the nanny.

As racism in South Africa was blatant, upfront, and obvious, I believed that because I could see it so clearly, I could avoid it. I believed I could live in the system but not be of the system. What I failed to understand or appreciate was how pernicious racism is. It seeps into your very being whether you are conscious of it or not. It was in me and with me—a constant chaperone making sure I abided by the rules and did not veer too far off the path of the social and political norms of the time. Like my mother before me, I treated my servants with kindness and generosity, with added respect. Despite my beliefs,

I was, however, because of my white privilege, still very much a part of the system.

I left South Africa when I could no longer abide by the racist policies I grew up with and did not want to risk my children growing up under this regime. I was also fearful of the rebellion and the blood bath that was threatening to come. My children's nanny, Anne Sharangwe, told me that she was glad we were leaving. She would never harm me or the children, but she could not account for the actions of the maid next door.

I find racism abhorrent, yet it lives within me, and from time to time, it gut-catches me unaware, and I am left dealing with this shadow aspect of myself. My reactions come unbidden and without thought. I find myself crossing to the other side of the street at the approach of a Black man; I will give five dollars to a Black person begging on the street when I would give one dollar to a white person. Am I compensating for my own racism?

I used to be caught by mild surprise when Black people attained positions of power, such as becoming heads of departments or mayors of large cities. Although this is no longer true, what is still true is that I often see colour first and person second—a lingering residue, I believe, of racism. I am embarrassed to talk about this. I offend my own values. It is as if my reactions have nothing to do with me, with my intelligent, rational self, yet they are my reactions. My gut reacts, and my head has to make sense of this. The reactions are slight, often just a twinge, but they are there.

I have a renewed appreciation for the ubuntu way of life. I see how it could carry me through dark and difficult times. It is not only racism I carry but also the values of ubuntu. On reflection, I am aware that I draw strength from the sweetness of character in the faces of the Black women who brought mothering comfort and support to my young self.

> *The redeeming quality of man lies in his ability to sense his kinship with all men. Yet there is a deadly poison which inflames the eye—making us see the generality of race, but not the uniqueness of the human face.*
>
> —Rabbi Abraham Joshua Heschel,
> Conference on Religion and Race,
> January 14, 1963

Father: The Storm Rolls In

It was a day like any other summer day. The sun was bright, the day was warm, and the thundering storm clouds that usually rolled in late afternoon were still some distance away. Trudging up the driveway with my heavy school case—switching it from hand to hand so as not to grow lopsided (school backpacks were a thing of the future) and looking forwards to a snack—I had no idea of the emotional storm that was about to roll over me.

The house was unusually quiet. There were no servants bustling about. Nobody hanging laundry, nobody sitting in the sun chatting over afternoon tea, and no dinner preparations underway. I walked through the silent, still kitchen to the dining room, where I heard muted voices. A couple of my mother's friends were there; the tone was hushed. The first words my mother said to me were "God took Daddy from us." My reaction was a strange one— not grief, not tears, not shock, but anger. I wanted to scream at God and at my mother.

I adored my father. He was a big bear of a man—over six feet tall, two hundred and twenty pounds, broad shouldered, and fit. He played squash, badminton, and golf. He was spirited, jovial, and kind. He was deeply in love with my mother. On cold winter mornings, he was known to call her from the office and say: "Ducks, stay in bed today. It is too cold to get up." Ducks was his pet name for her because she walked with her feet pointed slightly outwards, like a duck.

He was the glue that held the family together. He had a sunny personality and woke us up every school morning in a sing-song voice —Wakey, wakey, rise and shine"—and all was good with the world. He was the solid ground on which the family stood, the foundation on which we built our lives.

My father was my hero, the parent I was attached to. He encouraged and supported me. I was a tomboy; I did not gravitate to girlie things; I preferred playing cricket to playing with dolls. This was the 1950s; girls and women were not welcomed into traditional male sports. But I was a good player. My batting and bowling were as good as any boy's. I was an asset on any local neighbourhood pickup game. My father bought me a cricket bat and leg pads so I did not have to borrow them from one of the boys. He saw I had an aptitude for sports and had just begun to teach me to play golf.

I cherished those hours alone with him on the golf course. I could count on my father to take care of me, to comfort me, and to be there for me when I was afraid. Nothing bad could ever happen to me because he was there. But he died. He was forty-one. My mother was thirty-seven. My sister was twelve, and I was fifteen.

My father had been ill for some time. My sister and I were never told how ill he actually was and were given to believe that he was getting better. Tomorrow was always going to be a better day. Even when, at the end, he went into hospital, we were told he would be home soon. Except he did not come home, did he? He died. I was fifteen. Why wasn't I told?

My father died of stomach cancer. How could I have not known that he was so ill? There were no day or night nurses, no sick room atmosphere, no IV drips, no tubes, no pills beside his bed, and no signs that one associates with serious illness. He died, and I had no idea how ill he was. I learned later from an aunt that the first time he went into hospital, they had operated, but the cancer was so advanced they simply sewed him up again. I was fifteen. Why wasn't I told?

It was the 1950s, and compliance with social norms and patterns was expected, especially in South Africa, which was usually a decade behind the times. After World War Two, financial security was a prime focus. Men in our social circles were usually the main breadwinners. Women stayed at home and raised the children. Single mothers did not fare well. The social revolution of the 1960s was a decade away.

Cancer, or the big C, as it was called, was not talked about openly. There was much anxiety around it, as if you could catch it by merely mentioning it. Doctors were not upfront with their patients. It would not surprise me to learn that my mother herself had not been told and did not know how ill my father was or that some kind, well-meaning person advised her not to let the children go to the funeral. My mother was a victim of the times.

God had never featured in my growing up. It was pointless being angry at the god who never existed for me. So I turned my anger towards my mother— anger that lasted a long time. My relationship with my mother was not a good one from the beginning. I felt she did not like me. She probably loved me, but I do not think she liked me. I was not the daughter she wanted or needed. She would probably have preferred my namesake, Melanie Wilkes from *Gone with the Wind*, who was always a lady—kind, sweet, gracious, and considerate Melanie Wilkes. She got me instead: a rough-and-tumble, mouthy tomboy.

My anger, which was probably masking a pain I could not bear and any other feelings that might have been there, was further fuelled when my sister and I were not allowed to go to the funeral. We were left at home with the servants. They too should have been at the funeral. I recall feeling calm that day and somewhat out of it. There is a marvellous Afrikaans word that expresses how the day was for me—"dwaal," a combination of discombobulated, disconnected, ungrounded, and detached. In a fog. I was in a dwaal that day and probably for several weeks and months after that. I have wondered if my sister and I were given tranquilizers.

It rained heavily the day of the funeral. The servants told us that in African culture, it always rains at the funerals of great men. I found this comforting.

My relationship with my father carried on in my memories, fantasies, and dreams. His memory is a blessing. His absence still hurts.

Mother: From Anger to Forgiveness

My relationship with my mother sadly did not improve. I could not let go of my anger or forgive her for depriving me of the last months and days with my beloved father.

My poor, anxious, frightened, and distraught mother. This was not the first time death had shattered her life, nor would it be the last. Her life was in pieces. She was barely able to take care of herself, let alone a teenage daughter caught up in a thunderous, raging storm of anger and recrimination.

Forgiveness was a long way off.

> Too close
> too tight
> can't breathe.
> To live I must slip into darkness,
> die.
> To survive my death
> I must rage,
> rage dark
> red and black.
>
> Touch me, and you burn cold.
> I am the cold daughter
> the hot, raging cold one.
> What you needed I could not give,
> played dead to survive
> my death,
> forgetting it was all pretense
> I got lost in that dark
> dead place
> named depression.

Whatever my mother's life was like before she turned six, it was dramatically and tragically changed when her mother died of complications from childbirth. The placenta was not properly expelled, and her mother died from septicemia a month after giving birth. My mother, the eldest then of four children, had already lost a younger brother to diphtheria. Her father, my grandfather, could not raise the four children—aged six, four, two, and the month-old infant—on his own. He put them all into an orphanage, where he visited them on Sundays for a couple of hours. Their world had been turned upside down. All four children stayed in the orphanage until they turned sixteen.

My Mother as an Infant

Although my mother spoke lovingly with great warmth about friends and connections she made in the orphanage, she was painfully silent about her other experiences there. Her pain was as a silent scream—neither heard nor seen but still too present to ignore and too intense to touch. Through therapy, it became clear to me that as a child, I could not bear my mother's pain and was fearful that if I felt her pain, I would die. I carried this fearful child into adulthood.

But what about the fearful, anxious child my mother carried into adulthood?

As a child, I had no space for my mother's pain, yet I carried the burden of it, and it was a heavy burden. The message I got from my mother was that I was cold and selfish. She told me that even as an infant, I was cold. Did I freeze her out, even as a baby, because I knew intuitively that I could not bear the weight of her pain? If I saw it, touched it, or felt it, would it swallow me up, engulf me, and then kill me? My mother, who had been traumatized by the death of her brother and then her mother, needed so much more from me than I could give.

Despite the tragedies that befell her, my mother had a lust for life, and people enjoyed her company. She was beautiful, vivacious, and up for a social outing at any time. She was extroverted and fun to be with. A regular outing was a shopping trip downtown to John Orrs—an upscale department store with a fancy tearoom, where society ladies met for tea served with freshly baked scones, clotted cream, and homemade jam.

My mother's regular companion on these outings was her oldest friend Sonia. Two elegant and refined women who bickered loudly and with great passion about who was going to pick up the bill. They would reach across the table, grab the bill, or grab it out of each other's hands. It was a sport, a shouting match, a ritual to be repeated week after week. They were having fun. But I was embarrassed. To this day, I will never fight with anyone about who's going to pick up the bill.

My mother was always fashionably dressed. She was impeccably turned out, with matching bag, shoes, and gloves, with her hair coiffed. It was the 1950s, and you would not dare go downtown without gloves. Men were still wearing hats, but I have no memory of my mother doing so. My scruffy, unladylike tomboy ways and lack of interest in clothes or my appearance were a great disappointment to my mother. It would have been a delight and a pleasure for her to take me shopping.

My mother was well liked and well loved. She had a great capacity for friendship and kept the friends she made in the orphanage close; some of the friendships lasted eighty years. Only death separated them. Her friends could count on her loyalty and love.

Married to my father and living in her own home, my mother was safe and secure for the first time since age six. She was a gracious host, loved giving dinner parties, setting a beautiful table, and festooning the house with flowers. She was warm and welcoming to all.

My mother and father had been married for four years and had a two-year-old toddler, me, when the first of her siblings came to live with us. When each sibling turned sixteen and left the orphanage, they lived with us until they finished school or found jobs and were more independent and self-sufficient. Sometimes they would leave and come back.

I was about twelve or thirteen, and my mother's youngest brother was still with us. My mother, who had not been adequately mothered herself, did the very best she could with what little resources she had to mother and nurture her siblings. She would have mothered me in the same way, but I would not let her.

With the death of her beloved husband, my mother was forced to sell the family home in a hurry. There was no time for bargaining or waiting for the best deal. It was sold to one of my mother's father's stepchildren. There was no joy for my mother in selling her home to her stepsister, who had been raised by the father my mother had been deprived of.

My grandfather was remarried to a woman who ruled him with an iron fist. He was a man beaten down by tragedy and a difficult life and was easily manipulated. His second wife was not a nice person. She was nasty and jealous of her husband's previous children, whom she treated badly. Her own children, from an earlier marriage, were not particularly pleasant either.

We moved from our large home into a small two-bedroom apartment above a fish store. My sister shared the master bedroom with my mother. I had the small, dark bedroom at the back of the apartment. This took some considerable adjusting on all our parts.

My mother had not worked outside the home in seventeen years. In time and out of necessity, she found a job as a secretary and bookkeeper with a lovely Greek man, who owned a chain of shops, including the fish shop above which we lived. She worked diligently and without complaint in the small room behind the shop to support us.

My mother remarried when she was forty-six. Once again, she was safe and secure with a home of her own. But she was married for only a brief few years before her second husband died. He was operated on for a spot on his lung. It was benign, but he died from postsurgery complications in the car as my mother was rushing him back to the hospital.

This death was not even the last tragedy my mother would experience. Many years later, she was in a relationship with a wonderfully warm and caring man. We loved him and his children loved her. But this relationship was also doomed to end, with his untimely death.

My mother suffered a further loss when my sister and her husband emigrated to Canada, and soon after that, my first husband and I followed, with my mother's grandchildren, whom she adored and doted on. She was fifty-one when we left South Africa, still young enough to make a good life for herself in Toronto. When she was finally persuaded to join us, she was in her late sixties and could not adjust to a Canadian way of life. After nine months, she went back to South Africa for a visit and never came back.

She lived many more happy and settled years in South Africa, visiting Canada every year, well into her late eighties. She would arrive with her suitcases bulging, full of clothing for the grandchildren, homemade cookies, pickled herring, and all manner of South African goodies not available in Canada. Included in this bounty were many cans of salmon, which she believed—and continued to believe for many years—was unavailable in Canada.

My Mother with Her Younger Siblings

My mother's second husband was a judge in Germany who fled Nazi persecution during the Holocaust. Following the war, the German government provided monetary reparations for his loss of livelihood and property. On his death, this came to my mother. This, with the money he left her, enabled her to live reasonably well without having to go out to work again.

My mother was kind and generous, always ready with a helping hand for anyone less fortunate than herself. She was now free to serve those in need. At age eighty, she was still visiting the old and the sick; she would also drive old people, some of them considerably younger than herself, to their doctor's appointments and even to work.

Yet it was, regrettably, a very long time before my anger dissipated sufficiently for me to see the strong, caring, well-loved, and respected person my mother was. She overcame adversity after adversity and succeeded in creating a good and productive life for herself. She was loved by many and adored by her grandchildren and her great grandchildren.

I was born at 2:00 a.m., the hour when witches, demons, and ghosts are thought to appear and be at their most powerful. It is in the wee hours of the night when the offspring of Nyx, the Greek goddess of the night, come to visit, bringing with them their terrible accusations and judgments. Nyx was born of chaos and darkness and gave birth to doubt, guilt, blame, shame, rage, revenge, and despair.

The moon was full at the time of my birth. The Roman goddess Luna was riding her silver chariot across the dark sky. Luna? Lunatic? Does the full moon portend lunacy? Legend and even early science say that it does. However, many world mythologies represent the moon as wise and powerfully feminine, especially when full. She shines her soft light in the dark—that is, in the literal dark and the inner darkness, which is not visible in the strong, intense light of day.

I am drawn to the fantastical, mythological, mysterious, and magical and am driven to explore the dark side. It intrigues me to imagine that this has its roots in the full moon at the witching hour of my birth.

My gentle, sweet mother, who had known so much pain, did not and would not revisit that darkness. She distracted me from any pain and hurt I may have felt. If I were hurt and crying, she would say, "Don't cry. Look at the birdie" or "Don't Cry. Here's a sweetie." Not being allowed to have my pain made me feel unseen and angry. It took me a long time to understand that she truly believed she was trying to protect me.

May her memory be a blessing.

4. Brenda M. Doyle

Brenda M. Doyle has lived a succession of lives: nursing student, religious sister, teacher, childcare worker, psychotherapist, mother and grandmother, psychologist, world traveller, and, now, a fledgling writer. Her book, *The Therafields Psychotherapy Community: Promise, Betrayal, and Demise*, is available at Amazon and at Indigo.

Honouring My Mother

I grew up profoundly afraid of my mother, terrorized by her I have to say, but at such an early period of life that no clear memory remains. The nervous system holds it all. Here is a recurring dream from my earliest years. It is night. I am being chased by a shadowy figure along roads that twist and turn. I know that I will be killed if I am caught, but my legs seem to move too slowly. In my desperation, they betray me. I wake myself up. Another dream comes to me after years of psychotherapy: I enter a room in which a woman I know is standing alone. She beckons me to come closer to her. She is smiling. But as I approach and come closer, she suddenly reaches into her bosom, pulls out a knife, and moves to stab me. I resist her. I wake up bathed in terror. I am able to cry deeply and release pieces of that residual fear.

When I was a child, the fourth commandment to "honour your father and mother" was translated as an obligation of obedience to one's parents. Only much later did I understand its societal and political extensions: Obey those placed over one by a legitimate authority, ultimately God. Social engineering within a religious context—together with punishments, temporal or eternal for transgressions—has been an indoctrinating force in most societies while supporting worldwide patriarchy. In our more secular Western world, its power has been diluted considerably, exposing in a clearer light the enduring complexity of relations between children and their parents, citizens and their rulers, church members and their hierarchies, as well as men and women. Behind the injunction to honour has always lain the implicit warning of "or else."

As a child, I learned to honour my mother by obeying her, in good part because I found early on that not doing so would reap punishments better avoided. I was too undeveloped to appreciate and respect her as a person. Being a child, I needed her protection and so clung to her as would any other small being. I did not, however, have a feeling in my body of the love that flows from one person to another—a feeling that in those early days came from my father, a feeling that I have since experienced with others. Because that flow was not there between us, I could not trust that she stood solidly behind me. In time, I learned ways of hiding myself and my secrets from her, even as she and her secrets were hidden from me. Wordlessly, I knew her inner furies, belied though they were in the face with which she greeted the world. I eventually came to heartily dislike her, stung by the bitter and humiliating ways in which she would periodically lash out at me, the ways that she would put me down. As an adult, I saw her as little as possible, and while my dad was alive, I entertained notions of total parental divorce.

Such was my relationship with my mother until the last years of her life. She died in June, 2012, three months shy of her ninety-fifth birthday; she had spent almost twenty years a widow. After my dad's death in the fall of 1992, Mary (as I consistently thought of and called my mom in those days) continued to live in the comfortable two-bedroom condo that they had purchased in the Islington area after the sale of their long-time home in North Toronto. In the years that they spent together in Islington, my parents had made many friends in their building with whom they regularly socialized. Mary continued these relationships, meeting with people for drinks, dinner, and to play bridge. As long as my father was alive, I do not believe she missed the presence in her life for long periods of my brother, Craig, my sister, Valerie, and me. My older sister, Linda, had always welcomed her into the social web of her family and friends. Dad's companionship, scratchy though it sometimes was, Linda's attentions, and the acquaintances and society of her condo building sufficed.

A few months after Dad's death, however, Mary's sister and closest friend, Chick, died. That spring my younger sister, Valerie, who had had surgery seventeen years earlier for a melanoma at the back of her eye, was struggling with a recurrence. A second surgery stemmed the growth of her cancer, but within a few years, it clearly had not only continued to develop but also metastasized. After our father's death, Valerie had abandoned any show of tolerance towards our mother, whom she openly blamed for a host of painful indignities. In the late winter of 1997, Valerie was admitted to a palliative care hospice in Ottawa. Mary tried in various ways to contact her, but Valerie adamantly refused a connection. Knowing that she was close to death, Mary flew to Ottawa and simply appeared without warning at Valerie's bed side. Valerie called the nurse and asked to have our mother turned out. The nurse and a social worker talked with Mary in another room, telling her that there was nothing they could do to help her. Valerie's right of refusal was paramount. Mary returned to Toronto, devastated by the absolute, deathbed determination of her child to carry their estrangement to her grave.

I believe that this experience made cracks in the fairly rigid carapace of my mother's self-presentation. For some time before Valerie's death, within the family, Mary had characterized her as incomprehensible, indeed as "crazy." After her death, Mary would say that she could not understand what had gone wrong between herself and Valerie. "When she was a little girl," Mary would say, "she would run to me after her nap time, and we would cuddle together. How could those feelings between us have gone so awry?" I would listen to my mother's words and hear her confusion but would not venture to repeat the painful experiences that Valerie had told me about in her last few years. Until this juncture of her life, Mary, then eighty years old, had simply been defensive when confronted by implications of hurtful behaviour. Typically, she would go on the offensive, flaring up with not simply denials but with sharp words intended to quash her accuser. But Valerie's tough-minded refusal to give my mother absolution and comfort as she lay dying was an unending confrontation that she was unable to refute or to defend herself against.

In her eighties, I began to see Mary more frequently. Prior to that time, the occasions were rarely more than a family meal once or twice a year. But by then, I had a partner who liked her and was happy to accompany me to have dinner at her place or to take her out for a meal. It was never something that I liked or wanted to do, but I had become affected by a feeling of duty or of guilt—a sense that even if I did not enjoy spending time with my mother, I ought to visit her. Without my father's companionship, I knew that her life was poorer and more lonely, although at no time did she speak of anything so personal or revealing. In company with my partner (of whom she greatly approved), Mary played the good hostess or guest.

Only when she and I spoke by phone or on the rare occasions that we were alone together would she trumpet her opinions about how I or my daughters ought to be in the world. As the painful experience with Valerie sank to a deeper place within, though, Mary would sometimes temper her attack with the words "I blame myself. I know that I was too harsh with you, and now you have reacted by being too easy with your children." Her complaints tended to focus on issues like a ring that one of my daughters had had inserted into her nose or lip. In vain, I told her that my daughters' bodies belonged to themselves, and that even if I attempted to instruct or forbid them in these regards, they would do as they wished. I did not mention that they were simply not afraid of me in the way that I had been of her as a teenager.

The psychotherapy, particularly in the physical modality of bioenergetics, that I had received over a number of years had by this time helped me to overcome the depth of fear I had once experienced with my mother. I had gradually developed a capacity to speak back to her, countering her unpleasant sallies. These conflicts were difficult but considerably more rewarding than simply listening to her without comment and leaving in a rage. Once after such an exchange, she said to me, "I can't believe that you are so disrespectful towards your mother." I replied that respect is a quality that needs to cut both ways. If she was alright with hitting out at me in hurtful ways about things that were not her concern, then she should be prepared to hear that I did not like her way of speaking to me or her judgmental attitude towards my daughters. Struggles of this kind recurred over the years.

Often, they would conclude with my bringing the conversation to a close and not calling her for a few days. After a rupture between us, she would phone me and with a decided edge to her voice say something like, "I guess you don't want to hear my opinions, eh?" "That's right," I would say, and we would slide into conversing about one of our few areas of common interest— the Blue Jays. A couple of times I took her to a ballgame. She enjoyed seeing the spirited way in which I negotiated with a ticket seller outside the Skydome for our seats, and we had fun.

As the macular degeneration from which Mary suffered grew worse and her eyesight deteriorated, her balance was compromised. Generally, she got about very well, refusing the aid of a walker more out of pride than of a sense that one was unnecessary. Mary simply did not want people to know how old she was. Most of her pals in the building were ten or more years younger, but as she had always been youthful, they might not have realized the discrepancy. Throughout her eighties, Mary stayed in her Islington building, maintaining her routines and socializing with people whom she and Dad had befriended.

In the winter, she would rent a condo in Florida for a month, staying in the same place and getting acquainted with other expats who frequented the area. From time to time, she would travel more adventurously. Her last big trip was to Crete and to some Grecian islands. She was then, I believe, eighty-eight or eighty-nine. Stepping off the ship one day, she slipped and took a bad fall, fortunately not breaking any bones. Despite her ongoing balance difficulties, she continued to refuse the use of a walker or a cane. This was not her last misadventure. Once on a snowy day, she went off to see her hairdresser for what she characterized as "mission impossible." She slipped on a patch of ice, injuring her shoulder and hitting her head. She was never to regain full extension of that arm, a frustrating and progressively more limiting disability.

My sister Linda—who had trained as a nurse and who alone of Mary's children maintained an ongoing, amiable relationship with her—was concerned. Mary would walk down the rarely utilized back staircase of her condo building, slipping out to her grocery store. Linda worried that should she fall there, she might lie alone unattended for a long time. Moreover, Linda found on one visit that Mary had forgotten her boiling kettle, allowing it to burn dry. As she and her husband Darcy travelled each year to Florida for about six weeks, Linda became intensely worried that without her proximity, something catastrophic might happen.

She and Darcy began a concerted campaign to move Mary into a retirement building. Brochures were brought to her, arguments were marshalled, and visits to sites were arranged. Throughout, Mary fought against her relocation. As toughminded as she had always been, she eventually caved to their combined efforts. Her condo was sold; her money was invested; and she moved over to a one-bedroom apartment in a beautifully appointed, new residence. Briefly she appeared to enter the life of the building. It did not last. Soon she was complaining about the seating arrangements at regular meals served in the ground-floor dining room. Her allotted companions were not to her liking. She often requested to have her meals brought to her room. She did not make friends. Moreover, she discouraged the people with whom she had socialized in her former condo building from visiting her. She experienced her new situation as a humiliation and did not want to be seen by them in her reduced state. It became clearer that she had not experienced those with whom she had connected at her building as true friends—that is, people with whom one shares sufficient intimacy that life changes and problems can be spoken of and shared. Mary's capacity for the vulnerability of intimacy was limited.

From this time until her death three months before her ninety-fifth birthday, Mary continued to decline in every conceivable dimension. Although her constitution was strong, her body and health gradually deteriorated, as she refused to exercise or to involve herself in the activities of the residence. A few mini-crises took her to the hospital emergency department, where little could be done for her. In hospital, she complained to anyone who would listen about the "terrible service" she received. Her complaints at the residence were of the same nature. Within a couple of years, Linda and I, by then with joint legal responsibility for decisions related to her bodily needs, arranged to have her moved to a residence where she could receive more nursing care. She fought our decision, complicating the process for some months.

Soon after this move, Mary became essentially bedridden; she suffered a serious wound to her leg, occasioned by banging her ultrathin skin against a piece of the wheelchair, which she had begun to use. She had been determined to keep the foot flaps folded up so that she could propel herself along by her feet. She had been cautioned that she might thereby injure herself, but Mary did not easily take to advice. She had long felt herself to be the smartest person in the room, though when younger, she had been perhaps more diplomatic. Now, she did not bother to hide her thoughts. She railed against the "African" staff in the residence, who would serve "African" food like yams to her. She treated her caretakers brusquely, as if they were servants. Needless to say, they did not become fond of her. She refused to believe that the highly qualified doctor (also Black) who came to call was a real doctor, even after I had looked up his credentials for her online. She would not accept his diagnoses or his proffered treatments. She would be her own physician, thank you very much.

My mother was falling apart. A major shift took place in her treatment of Linda and me. Linda, who had over the years done so much for her, became the bad daughter—the one who was not with her enough and who was not sufficiently attentive to her needs. Linda ought to cancel dates that she had with friends for lunch or to play tennis in order to stand in constant attendance at her mother's bedside. Complaints, criticisms, and unpleasant confrontations began to pile up on Linda's increasingly confounded head. Her mother had always been her ally in the family; rarely did they disagree, and still more rarely would there be unpleasantness between them.

Mary was careful to deliver her broadsides when she had Linda alone. When Darcy or other family members were present, her language was more discreet. On one occasion, however, she did stray into disrespectful criticism in Darcy's presence. Linda had already told him of the way her mother had been speaking to her, and being privy to a clear example, he was enraged. He challenged Mary with the words, "How dare you speak that way to my wife, your daughter, who has been so kind to you." He then escorted Linda out of the room and out of the building. Mary's abuse towards Linda was by no means attenuated, but she perhaps became more careful about the context.

With a new bad daughter, Mary needed a good one, someone she could draw close, flatter, and confide in. That became my new position. Just as Linda was reeling from having been cast out of favour, I marvelled at my own sudden elevation to grace. Linda, Craig, and I had a few conversations that were enlightening, particularly to Linda. Previously, when we had spoken of treatment we had endured from Mary, Linda would have little to say. Perhaps, she simply could not believe what we were telling her. Now, she got it. It was a good feeling for me—maybe even from the perspective of all-too-satisfying revenge. Okay, I wore it, and now you are having to take it. Join the circle!

The three of us began to gain a greater sense of camaraderie about the ongoing problem that was our mother. We talked more and developed collaborative ways of being with and seeing to her needs. At the time, I was still working quite a bit. Moreover, I spent each weekend at our cottage in Orillia. I lived in downtown Toronto, a thirty-minute drive to Mary's building. Linda, in contrast, lived within five minutes of Mary and was not working. She had been a nurse; she was considerably more domesticated than I was when it came to many of the practical details of life, and she had had the long-time habit of helping my mother with shopping trips. I considered myself ever so fortunate, as Mary's need for greater care evolved and was taken up primarily by Linda. With the new dispensation in which Mary parcelled out her smiles and favours, however, I clearly needed to step up to the plate. I had lived with a degree of guilt for some time, knowing that Mary's care had been essentially left up to my sister.

For most of the summer, Linda and her family lived at their cottage on Christie Lake near Perth. She was back and forth to Toronto for various occasions during the summer and likely came more often those years to check in on her mom. I began to visit more frequently. I would squeeze in a brief visit between sessions with my clients, though it would entail an hour's driving. The Mother, as Craig and I then referred to this personage, was bedridden and would tend to tire quickly.

I would slip into her darkened room, careful not to waken her; the television was always on the CBC news channel. When she would become conscious of my presence, we would share a greeting; I would lean over to kiss her soft, pale cheek, and she would say, "It is so good to see you, dear." I might perform some slight task for her: opening the ubiquitous bottle of extra-strength Tylenol with which she liberally medicated herself, refreshing her water glass, or fishing about in her bedclothes for her ever disappearing telephone. I would hear her current complaints, or, on a better day we would talk about the Blue Jays' progress that season. Soon she would say, "It was so good of you to come, dear." This was my cue to leave. She did not want visits of any length. I would leave exhaling as I headed down the hall, happy to get away and back to my own life, all the while feeling progressively greater sadness for this once powerful woman who did not have the capacity to either live or die.

Craig began visiting her more often as well. For years, he had been unpredictable in his contact, sometimes available, often absent for months at a time, neither calling nor answering her calls to him. He began a weekly routine of visiting The Mother in her Eglinton Ave. retirement residence, later at the more-or-less Lawrence and Weston Road nursing home. He would sit quietly with her and never contradict her complaints or statements, since he had a long experience with its fruitlessness. Over time, two things began to happen. The first was that she would sometimes ask him something about his teaching. A born storyteller, he could wax eloquent about European wars and politics in the twentieth century. Having lived through this terrain and being a political junkie herself, she was enthralled by his knowledge. She began to mention to me how smart Craig was. It seemed to be a revelation to her that he was so well versed in history. It was an unfortunate thing that she discovered only at the very end of her life that her child was an interesting and personable man—unfortunate for her and for Craig.

I also came in for more respect and attention. My mother had disapproved of many of my life choices and had never tasked herself with constraining the expression of her opinion. I had taught in a high school for a few years. This was clearly considered a respectable position with bragging possibilities because her friends were so informed. When I left teaching to work full time as a psychotherapist, she told no one of this less conventional option. Later, when I went to graduate school preparing to become a psychologist, she frowned and discouraged me several times. "You should go back to teaching," she would say. "You would have a good salary and could give your daughters a proper lifestyle."

"What do you mean by that?" I would ask, truly surprised. "You could get a cottage"— presumably like my sister had. It meant nothing to her that the relative poverty that I lived in during graduate school was a choice that I had freely embraced because I loved the program that I was in, the things I was learning, and the future that I saw for myself. When I graduated after five years, her friends heard by accident about my degree and were laudatory and excited. Suddenly, I became a wonderfully presentable product. She would call to tell me that I could be her doctor now. She wanted to consult me about what she had self-diagnosed as depression and wondered what I would recommend. I agreed that she did suffer from depression and likely had for decades. I would talk with her and make recommendations with which she would agree but never follow.

All her life my mother had resisted telling stories about her family or her past. When I would question her about, for example, her childhood on the farm, she would counter with: "Why do you want to know about that?" On more than one occasion she told me that I was weird. Regular or normal people did not ask such questions or talk about such things. "Stay away" was her clear message. Yet in the last year or so of her life, my mother began to remember and to think about incidents long gone, and wonder of wonders, she began to tell Craig about them and then me. The first story had to do with a period when she and my dad would have been in their fifties. They had socialized with close neighbours, a community that gradually expanded to others from adjoining streets.

In this process, they met a man who had briefly been a boyfriend of my mother's before she met Dad. And, thrilling to say, there still existed a spark between them, or, perhaps, the spark was rekindled. I believe that she saw him a few times outside of their social group. At first, the story seemed to be that there had been some hanky-panky between them, although later she hastened to deny that—not wanting my brother and I to judge her as a bad woman. Hardly! There was a clear indication in the tale, however, that she had enjoyed that moment in time—in part as an affirmation of her own womanly charms but also in some fashion as a reprisal for what she considered Dad's flirtatious or perhaps even philandering ways. No further details were forthcoming, and the topic was dropped. But "Wow," Craig and I exclaimed to one another, a little window into the lives of the parents! Who would have thought?

More powerful and far more revealing was the second revelation that Mom made to us. (By this point I had changed my way of thinking of and speaking to and of her.) On the phone, she told me that in her life, she had never been able to cry, not even when my dad had died. Thinking about the way that she had held in her vulnerable feelings, she had suddenly remembered being sexually molested by her mother's younger brother when she was five or six. This uncle lived while unmarried in the farmhouse next door, with his parents and other siblings. Mom and her younger sister Chick would go there sometimes to be taken care of, and the uncle would take them upstairs to his room. Any still lingering resentment or anger that I harboured fell away in the moment of hearing her story. I felt so badly for her. I also had been sexually abused as a young child, so knew well the depth of emotional devastation that an experience of this kind could have. At once, so much of my mother's life became open to me, answering the question that her older sister, Alma, would put to me every now and then: "What could have happened to your mother to make her the way that she is, for her to treat people the way that she does?" We did not speak more about this memory. It might have come to her and then receded as she moved closer to shutting down mentally, emotionally, and physically.

Other pieces of her early life that I had known about also began to have greater relevance for me. When she was about two years old, the Spanish flu pandemic, which killed more people than the world war that had just concluded, struck her family. No one died, but all were deathly ill. It was a story commonly told in her family that Mom, just a baby, seemed to intuit that no one was able to care for her during those desperate days, so she simply lay quietly in her crib until people regained their strength. What could this have been like for a two-year-old? Was she also so ill that she had not the strength to cry out, or did she cry to the point that she gave up and resigned herself to being abandoned? Another piece: When she was about nine, her sister Leola, the next oldest in the family, finished grade eight and then remained at home to help her mother with the younger children and the care of the household. I believe it likely that Mom did not take kindly to Leola, since she had responsibility over her. As an adult she had nothing to do with Leola and her family, although she remained close to Chick and in fairly good connection with Alma.

Towards the end, Mary was but a little bird of a creature, scarcely able to hold up her head as her body struggled to let go. When she was finally able to die, I rejoiced. I could not bear any longer to watch her slow progress towards the oblivion for which she longed. The last years of her life were painful and difficult for our entire family, most of all for her. But the blessing that came for me in this period was a deeper introduction to and understanding of the woman who had given me life, her excellent genetic codes, and who as a mother had given as much as she had to give. While she was invulnerable and controlling, I had heartily disliked her, but when she could no longer keep her painful memories at bay and to herself, I became able to know and care for her and to honour her for the strengths that she had possessed.

My Mother at Twenty-Seven Years Old

Parents and Parenting

> They fuck you up, your mum and dad.
> They may not mean to, but they do.
> They fill you with the faults they had
> And add some extra, just for you.
>
> But they were fucked up in their turn
> By fools in old-style hats and coats,
> Who half the time were soppy-stern
> And half at one another's throats.

—Philip Larkin

These first two stanzas of Larkin's poem brought me to another story even as I thought about my parents. It is about my own parenting, about how I, like my parents, entered into the fray of childcare just as limited, just as flawed, and just as divided between my own needs and those of my children as were they. Their parents had put upon them the burdens of their generation, as had the parents of the previous one—and so on back into prehistory.

I am no longer interested in blaming my parents for the things that they foisted onto me. I am more aware of the struggles of their childhoods and of the cores of pain with which they lived their lives. But now, more to the point, I am humbled and pained by the recognition of ways that I hurt my own children, particularly Betha, my older daughter. She and I have spoken quite openly for a number of years about the early troubles in our relationship. Betha would say how she grew up feeling alone—feeling that there was no one who had her back. I know that when she was a baby and a toddler, I experienced depression and that with her I reenacted some components of the relationship that I had very early with my own mother.

When she was born, I was delighted and happy with my lovely baby. But by the time she was only a few months old, I had sunk into postpartum depression and was unable to feel anything towards her. I knew that I loved her but could no longer feel it. My husband and I were living in a communal home, part of the Therafields psychotherapy community that I had joined ten years earlier. I spoke about my trouble in a house group session. No comment was made; no proposal was suggested to help me. I did not have my own individual therapist at the time with whom to take up this problem; perhaps, people did not realize that. I assumed that my failure of feeling was seen as a personal flaw, as it was not addressed. Depression was not at all well understood or identified within my community despite its psychodynamic orientation. It was over twenty years later that this recurrent condition from which I suffered was diagnosed and treated. I simply struggled on, trying to do my best.

Betha and Me

I have a picture of Betha, taken when she was about ten months old. In it, she looks withdrawn and unhappy. My husband's sister visited around that time. She said to him that she thought Betha was not thriving, and I knew that it was true. When I was pregnant and we were married, I had had an image that when the baby came, I would hold her in my arms and that my husband would literally be behind me, holding me in turn. His strength would augment my strength. But in the event, it was never like that. He was not around much in those days. He was always working, and he had a room of his own. The baby was entirely mine to care for. I was tired a lot and could be irritable. I was living together with the baby, my husband, and others in our large, communal house but actually was living as likely I had done for much of my life—basically alone. The difference was that in that alone space, my daughter was with me. I was alone and so was she.

I find it painful to go towards these memories. The nights were the most difficult. For the first few months, Betha slept well, waking once for a feeding but falling right back to sleep again. Then she began a different pattern, waking to be fed but no longer sliding back asleep. I did not know what to do. I had no one to care for the baby when I was desperate to sleep myself. It never occurred to me to press my husband into being involved during the nights or even to articulate to others how I was struggling. I somehow assumed that because I was a mother, I ought to know intuitively how to deal with every problem. I would bring Betha into my bed and try to go back to sleep, but restless, she would move about or crawl all over me. In my exhaustion, I would feel totally oppressed by her. I would try to shake her off. I hardly even knew what I was doing.

Once during the winter, when Betha was about a year and a half, we were staying with some people in a shared vacation house in Florida, another place owned by our community. The house was full. Betha and I were given a room that had been made from half of a former garage, and we slept together on a mattress on the floor. Because there was no window, when the light was off, the room was entirely dark. It was a struggle for both of us to get to sleep. The place felt creepy. One day, Betha and I were playing on the front lawn. I ran a bit away from her and then towards her. I saw on Betha's face that she became afraid of me when I did this, but I did it a second time. I knew immediately that I was deliberately frightening her, and it shocked me.

I never did anything like that again, but also, I did not talk about this with anyone. My relationship with my husband was rocky, and I did not have enough trust in my companions to talk about the kind of aberration that I had felt. I already thought badly enough about myself, and I feared being judged and talked about as a bad mother—a label then freely being flung at other women in our community. I still have pictures of Betha from that time in Florida. In them, she looks so forlorn. I could never throw those pictures away because I did not want to lose touch with the child that she was then and the knowledge that I had of frightening her.

When my second child was born, Betha was almost four. Our family moved north to one of the Therafields' farm properties about six months later. Being with the new baby was much easier for me, although the year and a half that we lived in the country was difficult. My husband left to go to Toronto to work about 6:30 a.m. and returned in the early evening. During that long winter, I had no car and no companion. When my husband got home, I would hand over the kids and go outside to pace up and down the snow-bound driveway—anything just to get away. If he was out in the evening as well, my frustration and irritability could easily turn on Betha. I would put her to bed, longing for time to myself, but sometimes she would come to the head of the stairs and want me to come up again. There were times that I simply yelled at her to go back to bed. I wanted to be left alone.

We returned to our home in the city the following August. The baby, Catherine, was then two; Betha was almost six. Once again in a communal home and with some young women interested in being with the girls, I was able to find time for myself. I began to take preparatory courses for graduate school. I loved my studies and the direction I felt myself moving along. The children went to a Montessori school on the Toronto island—Betha right away, Catherine after one year.

Having our children changed me and my husband in ways that led us away from each other. I had become somewhat more self-assured, more solidly grounded in myself, less dependent on him. He had gradually become focused on the children. He worried about their safety often in situations that did not warrant concern. He would say that he didn't like to be out of contact with them for more than a few hours. This preoccupation had a detrimental impact on our relationship, adding another layer of difficulty to other, longer-standing issues. The connection between us became bracketed within a Wednesday evening dinner out and a Sunday afternoon movie. Conversation was about the children and about his ideas for retirement. He would say, "I've lived my life," and I would reflect to myself, "Mine has hardly begun." But I struggled to keep my thoughts and desires in line, trying to be the so-called good woman proscribed by my community.

One of the courses that I took a year after we returned to Toronto had a definitive impact on me. Our community had managed to elude the ongoing women's movement. The readings in this course thrust me directly into the movement, and in them, I read myself and my history. Animated with new perspectives and galvanized by the success I was gaining in my schooling, I could no longer repress my longings for a life of greater freedom.

It was at that time that I separated from my husband, and essentially left the Therafields' bubble. After our first confrontation in which I told him I could no longer continue with our marriage, the next steps were unclear. I asked him to leave our home, but he refused, saying that he was not going to leave the kids. If I wanted a separation, I could leave. All our income came from his teaching position. The possibility of moving into another home with the children never occurred to me. I slept in a bed in the kids' room for about a month, but the tension in the house was stifling. My husband and I were both clear that we wanted our kids to have both parents solidly in their lives. With his agreement and our joint bank account, I rented a basement apartment two blocks away and moved there. The sense of joy I felt in my new, basic, and slightly shabby unit was immense. I felt free as never before. It was the first time I had a place entirely to myself. But there were, of course, repercussions.

Catherine did not seem to register the changes in the household, but Betha was terribly distraught by the separation. When I told her that her dad and I had decided to part, she burst into tears, saying that she did not want to lose her daddy, as had happened to a friend of hers. I assured her that she was not going to lose anyone and that both her parents loved her and would always be with her. But the transition was difficult. Her attention at school greatly lessened. Her teacher told me that while there she would sometimes go over to her little sister, put her arms around her, and cry. It was painful.

I was at the house all day, every day that first year and most days after that for many years. At 7:00 a.m., I would take over as my husband left for school. I got the kids up, dressed, fed, and drove them to the ferry docks for their ride with other kids and the teachers across to the school. At noon, I would pick up Catherine and at about four, Betha. I did my own schoolwork while at the house, but I also did the laundry, got the groceries, and made supper. After the kids went to bed, I would go down to my own little place.

When I look into the spaces of my relationship with Betha over those early years, I find myself looking into my mother's face. It is as though my mother was there within me and with Betha. I have early memories of being held lovingly by my father but not even one of that nature with my mother. In my mother's look, I felt that I was an unasked-for burden that was resented. She punished me in little mean ways that I could not understand. And at another level, I was afraid of her. My sister, nineteen months older than me, was ten when our younger sister was born. She became Mom's ally and helper.

The latter told me once that she started spanking her own kids when they were about six months old. "If they are old enough to cry for nothing, they're old enough to be spanked," she said. That brusque, hands-on, and no-nonsense attitude was certainly characteristic of our mother's sister Alma, ten years older than her, who when she finished grade school stayed at home to be my grandmother's helper with my mother and her three siblings.

I was surprised and shocked by my sister's words about spanking her children when they were so young. There was a lot of spanking, slapping, and yelling in our family as I grew up—in the early years primarily by my mother. Still, I had not yet connected that statement with the fear of my mother so deeply lodged within me until I was well into middle age. In the early years of my parents' marriage, my father was a travelling salesman and away during the work week. My mother was basically alone with two babies, then a third, and a house to care for. She had had her own traumas as a young child, which were never spoken of until the last year of her life. Not a natural mother, she gave us what she had, as too much of it reverberated from her own early experiences.

One clear memory that stands out from when I was about three or four is of being forcibly held upside down on my back, arms pinned to my body, by my father over the kitchen sink, with my head down under the water so that my mother could wash my long hair. I struggled and screamed and cried, certain that I was about to be drowned. Undoubtedly, I had resisted having my mother wash my hair in the bathtub. She must have told my father that it had to be done that way, and he did not contradict her in those days—only much later when we had all gone our own ways did they irritate each other. To this day, I experience a rising sense of panic if physically constrained against my will.

Fear of my mother co-exists with the other feelings I have of her, my father, and my siblings. My mother was closed off from a capacity for touching and feeling others. In some ways with my own small children, I lived an isolated life, often one of depression and frustration, unable to connect in a deeply meaningful way with the people around me. I just kept on going, putting on a good-enough face to get by. But much of life felt like pushing a heavy stone up a hill. Catherine, a cheerful, easy little baby, seemed to be fine. Betha was not. In some manner, she also lived in the place of unhappiness that I inhabited. My mother was me; I was my mother to Betha. I did not spank my kids, but when Betha was about eight, on several occasions when frustrated with her, I slapped her arm. She would cry, and I felt guilty about each occasion. The third time, I told her that I was sorry, that I knew that hitting her was wrong, and that I did not want to do it again. Admitting to Betha and to myself that it was a harmful way to deal with my frustration allowed me to get past that temptation.

There was another experience that had greatly affected how I felt about myself. When I was six, we moved to Ottawa. Two years later, the young uncle of one of my playmates on our street invited me to sit on his knee and then sent my friend out of the room for something. In her absence, he slipped his hand into my clothing, touching my genitals. My entire body and my brain instantly exploded with the most pleasurable sensation of my young life. He whispered into my ear, "You like that, don't you?" Later, he gave me a nickel, promising to give me a quarter another time, and instructed me that what had happened was a secret between us.

I did not know or understand what had happened. I had no words for it. I intuited that there was something bad about it, something I could never mention to my parents. Sometime afterwards, I went again to the house, but my friend and her family were out. The uncle said that he had the promised quarter for me. "It's in my room," he said. "Just come up stairs, and we'll get it." His room was in the attic of the house, reached only by a ladder inside a hallway closet. As I preceded him up the ladder, I became nervous. Once there, he told me to get onto the bed. I did so, but by then, I knew something was wrong, and I was really scared. He paced up and down in the room for a moment or two, but then yelled at me to leave. I did so, as fast as I was able, never returning to that house again.

But I had been thrust into an area of sexual experience that though secret and bad was nonetheless compelling. I began to experiment with a couple of children my own age, forays that were never satisfyingly productive. When my family moved to another city about a year later, I determined that I would leave those experiences behind, feeling by then that they were shameful and dirty. I was able to do that, but their power and impact had gone deeply into my sense of myself and would reemerge over the following decades in a variety of ways. In the meantime, I had been catapulted out of childhood and into a place where my fractional knowledge of adult sexuality, albeit twisted in nature, prematurely separated me from my cohort and in some ways from everyone. I suddenly knew something about men, something I could sense in some—something I came to despise, even as I despised myself. And then there was the Church's teachings, which in time handicapped me with a sense of sin and potential damnation.

Over time living with my father's expressions of depression and frustration added another dimension of unhappiness for me. My memories from when I was very young were of a loving, wonderful daddy whom I adored and with whom I felt safe. But along the line, things changed. When we moved to Ottawa, my dad had a new job, which did not require his travelling. He was with us daily, a different life for him and for us. During the years in which he was travelling our week had had two parts: Monday to Friday with Mom and whomever she might have had to help with her home and babies; and Friday evening, Saturday, and Sunday with a dad who was happy to be with us, who sang in his lovely tenor voice, and who played with us.

All together, we weathered the workdays and the weekends in Ottawa. There were great times then, like swimming and a picnic supper at a beach after his summer workday. Within a couple of years, though there were changes. My younger sister was born. I had my own hidden secret experiences that I could never speak of. My father's mother had died, although it was barely spoken of, and he was experiencing frustration over the limitations of his job. His boss owned the small company he worked for, so there was no place for him to move up. He seemed more remote to me. I also sensed his growing special relationship with my older sister.

Mental health issues had dug a deep trough through my dad's family. His mother, of whom he never spoke, was a difficult person. She had come from another farming family; her father was a serial drunk who would beat his wife and children when frustrated. She was a beautiful and clever woman, strong in her Catholic faith and values but brutal in the demands she made upon my father. In her fifties, she was hospitalized at least twice after what must have been suicide attempts. As a teenager, my uncle would sometimes have to sleep on the stairs leading from their apartment to prevent her from going out at night to try again. She was successful when I was about six, escaping the family bounds and drowning herself in the swift-flowing river that bisected their small city. Only as an adult was I told all this by a second cousin.

Our family lived in another small Ontario city when I was between ten and fourteen. It was there that I first experienced an irrational attack from my father. I came into the house one day alone. Everyone was out except him. He was sitting in a chair in the living room sunken into a dark mood. As I passed by in the hall, I said something to him, something quite innocuous. He leapt from his chair and ran after me into the kitchen. I tried to flee but was trapped in the small pantry off to the left. There he hit me so hard on the side of my head that I was knocked out. The next thing I knew I was lying on the kitchen floor with him standing over me, still in a state of rage. He said not a word but kicked me in the side and walked away, leaving me crying. I cried in pain but also from humiliation and with a sense of being despised by my father.

Over the next years, until I was able to leave my parents' house, he would periodically hit me again in this manner if annoyed. Just one very hard clout on the side of the head, sometimes when my back was turned, and I was not expecting it. I would literally see stars. For years as a young woman, I could not sit in a restaurant, for example, with my back to the door. My back and neck would tingle with warning—my body's notification of fear that something or someone dangerous might come from behind. When I walked under signage on the streets, I had an uncomfortable sensation across the top of my head, as if the overhang were about to fall on me. It was a long time before I connected these fears and sensations with my father's punishments. I knew that he did not treat my two sisters in this way. When he was annoyed with my younger brother, he would more likely kick him in the behind.

I have a sense of long passages in my life influenced centrally by my need to retreat from what many would consider normal life. As a teen, I retreated from family life and the demands of school by reading historical novels extensively and later by playing basketball. I got away from my parents' home by entering the nursing school of a hospital hundreds of miles away. It was a respectable placement, and it did not require more than simply completing grade twelve to qualify. I retreated from long-standing sexual and religious confusion, which was reactivated by my immersion in a Catholic hospital milieu, by going into the novitiate of the religious order running the school. Four years later, I managed to extricate myself with the help of a priest counsellor who intuited rightly that I had not chosen religious life freely as a vocation.

During those years of adolescence and young adulthood, depression and loneliness were often my companions, but although I lost, I also gained from the choices that I made. My scholastic grades were poor, and became poorer each year during high school, but I gained enormously from the reading that I did, as it engendered in me an interest in history and later in travelling the world. Basketball and other sports kept my body healthy and were a prime source of catharsis. I was not terribly interested in the nursing curriculum, but the intense eight hour shifts on the medical and surgical wards with other young women were surprisingly interesting and rewarding. I learned a lot. While in the novitiate, I used available high school texts to teach myself six grade thirteen courses. I took the final exams at a local school to qualify for the university courses that my congregation wanted me to take, surprising and delighting everyone, including myself, with the high marks I attained. I had discovered the love and joy of learning.

While I was away, my family moved to Toronto, so after leaving the convent, I returned to its bosom, though not for long. Peace between my mother and me was short lived, although my father by that time clearly saw me as an adult and respected my capacity for making choices. I had spent two years at university while with the religious order but needed another year to complete my university degree. Before long, I met a couple of girls from my nursing school who invited me to move in with them, found a part-time job, got a student loan, and registered at the University of Toronto.

During those early years in Toronto, I dealt with my family relations primarily with avoidance. For the first year or so, I would attend the de rigeur Sunday dinners at my parents' home, together with my brother and two sisters, one of whom was by then married with two infants. The visits were fairly antiseptic: have a drink, enjoy your meal, and go home. No conversation of note. After I became involved in what became Therafields, my visits became considerably less frequent. In my late forties, with the help of bioenergetic therapy, I was freer and clearer about the reasons for my intense discomfort when with them. This clarity only made the experiences that much more acutely painful.

At my father's seventy-fifth birthday dinner, I found that I could barely stomach the superficiality of the conversation. I wanted to shout out my unhappiness with our relationships. I determined later that evening that, cost what it might, I would tell my parents things that I had held back for decades. In the morning I called and asked if I could come over to talk with them. "Yes, come over," they said. We sat in the living room. I wanted to avoid hysterics of any kind or outright blaming, so I began by telling them that I had always felt apart in the family, separate from the others.

I told them then about my experience of sexual molestation. At this, my mother moved over from her chair, sat beside me on the couch, and put her hand on my shoulder in sympathy. I went on to say that I believed she had always been closer to my older sister and that she had judged me as lesser because I followed different a lifepath. I then spoke about the effects of my father hitting me so powerfully on the head. My mother leapt to her feet and said that those things had never happened, that I was consumed with jealously of my sister, and that she was not going to be blamed for my miserable life. With that, she stalked upstairs to prepare for an outing with a friend.

I sat quietly for a few minutes taking all of that in. I asked myself if it was true that I was jealous as charged. No, I knew that my sister and I were different from one another. She had chosen her ways and I, my own. I followed my mother upstairs. Clearly, I was not so frightened of her as I had been. She sat with her back to me at her dressing table, scolding me once again for wasting my time in graduate school. "I'm happy with what I'm doing," I told her. She gradually cooled down, finished getting ready, and we went downstairs, where I was introduced to her friend, and off they went.

I sat down with my dad. He said to me with tears in his eyes, "I don't remember the things you were talking about, but if I hurt you, I am sorry." I could feel that he meant it sincerely, and it helped me to begin to let go of the anger that I had held against him for so long. I drove home feeling quite satisfied with my foray into telling truth to power. I had begun a reconciliation with my father, and I had not been so frightened of my mother that I had to head into a fight with her. I had said my piece and knew that I could do it again if circumstances warranted.

And of course they did.

My father died six years later. During the two decades that my mother lived as a widow, I gradually became more involved with her and understood how the traumas she experienced early on curtailed her capacity to connect lovingly with people in her orbit. Learning about the syndrome of depression and being treated for it by antidepressants in my early fifties were essential for my being able to let go of the difficult things that had happened between my parents and me over the years.

Betha escaped our family by going to a university outside of Toronto. It was not a great year for her. Lots of partying, lots of sick time, not a lot of good marks. Afterwards, she announced that she wanted to move to Vancouver, where a few of her pals had already settled and were working. I was against the idea at first, although I later saw that it was something that she just had to do. Over the years, she took jobs that paid the rent and had a couple of boyfriends with whom she lived. She came to Toronto periodically, and I met with her several times in Vancouver, San Francisco, and Miami.

At twenty-seven, she became pregnant. After her baby was born, tensions with the baby's father led to a separation about a year and a half later. It was a difficult time for her. She could not get daycare until the child was two years old, but without it, she could not work to support herself and the baby. I encouraged her to come back to Toronto, where social services were much better for single mothers and where she had her family to help her. She came, moving in with Catherine for about a month. In the meantime, she got free daycare for her baby, an apartment, and a job as an office manager.

Two years of running an office motivated Betha to aim higher. She got a student loan and entered a four-year degree program in psychology at Ryerson University. She was an excellent student, on the dean's list yearly, and was psychology student of the year in her third year; she was even given a summer lab job usually awarded only to graduate students. She royally proved herself! Afterwards, she took a job as office manager with a newly opened clinic for addicts while also taking courses in addiction counselling and learning on the job to lead groups and counsel individuals. She became accredited as an addictions counsellor. After about six or seven years with our family in Toronto, she and her daughter moved back to Vancouver so she could take a job in the sector dealing with addiction there.

The time that she and her daughter spent with me and the others in Toronto was precious for all of us. For four years during that period, Catherine, together with her two children, lived in the ground floor apartment of my home. We had a weekly family dinner together, and Betha's daughter stayed overnight once each week. In the beginning, many remnants of the problems between Betha and me would surface. By that time, however, we had both matured somewhat, and were more able to articulate the issues we were unhappy about. Besides, her daughter was a common rallying point for us. When Betha began seeing a few individuals dealing with addictions for counselling, she sought my help in understanding their problems. We developed a sincere respect for one another's work. Our time together laid the grounding for a deeper connection and a capacity to talk openly with one another. It was never perfect, but it has grown and continues to grow between us.

Betha now works with the most marginalized people of the Vancouver downtown east side. They are homeless and addicted to substances that can and do kill them. Each month, people whom she has known, worked with, and cared for die on the streets of Vancouver. She is passionately committed to them. She knows them from the inside out. Some years ago, she acknowledged that she herself had a drinking problem. She found the strength to quit drinking and to separate from her partner of several years who was unwilling and unable to stop.

My daughter has gained a reputation in Vancouver for her clarity of vision with respect to needed changes in policy and funding in the treatment of addictions. I see the future that will be hers as this area of service must, of necessity, be expanded not just in Vancouver but across our country. I am proud of her, of her work, and of the manner in which she has been able to address and work with her own troubles. We talk regularly and openly about ourselves and our work. For this, I am so entirely grateful.

I have had to face my guilt over the past, over the ways that I frightened and inhibited my daughter when she was young, and over the legacy that she was forced to take on from the impact of my family on my own young life. As I have been able to let go of my anger against my parents, been able to understand their troubles, and been able to forgive and care about them, I have found myself standing in a location where I can both acknowledge the harm that I have done and forgive myself.

Philip Larkin is right in his declarations that our parents fucked us up and that they themselves were fucked up by their parents. But the last stanza of his poem is not a satisfying or necessary conclusion:

> Man hands on misery to man,
> It deepens like a coastal shelf.
> Get out as early as you can
> And don't have any kids yourself.

Having and raising children is unquestionably one of the most, if not the most, challenging endeavours in life, but it can also be its most rewarding. We never get it right. We always mess up because we are far from being a perfect anything. The recognition of our mistakes, of even our abuses, is difficult and painful. Standing in a central location between our parents and our children, we can look and feel in both directions. Humbled by our own insufficiencies, we can more easily understand and forgive those of our parents. In a less judgmental space, we might also move towards a healing place of forgiveness of ourselves, the sine qua non of health and peace.

5. Kathy Honickman

Kathy Honickman is a retired French, special education, and drama teacher of thirty-eight years. She has always had a love of writing. As a student, she lived in Paris, where she developed a greater understanding for the nuances of communication through language. Later, as a teacher, she wrote, directed, and produced many plays and presentations for children. For several years, she wrote a popular weekly newspaper column called "Parenting" about the trials and tribulations of being a young, working mother of two precious children. Since 2000, Kathy has pursued her passion for memoir by compiling hundreds of pages of historically researched family stories and by attending postsecondary institutions, both as a student and cofacilitator. In addition to her devotion to the arts, Kathy loves spending time with her husband, children, and grandchildren at "Spa-Baba."

Maybe I Shouldn't Be Telling You This

Please don't die Mum.
Not in rush hour.
Can you hear me? I have to whisper.
I bet they already think I'm a moron.
Especially the ambulance attendants. What are they,
twenty?
I made such a fuss so they'd lift you gently. Even made them
turn the radio off.
And that caregiver, Dolores? Denise? Since she met
Marilyn, I get the cold shoulder. So, what else is new?
It's as if you put out some kind of vibe.
Or maybe there really is something wrong with me?
Like I always thought?
I don't know.
Anyway, who's here now?
Me, right?
Your senior citizen, broken-down daughter, that's who.
Even though you brought Marilyn and me up like twins,
I'm a year older, so it's my job.
My job to take you in, lug you upstairs to the sitting room,
saturate your sandpaper skin with cream, keep the supply
of audiobooks and Ensure and visitors coming.
My job never to show too much happiness as the last petals
of life fall off your withered stem.
Yup, another one of those times when I'm the oldest. And
only when you're ready, a coma only days away, but we
don't know that yet, was it okay to take you back to your
condo. And even then, it's still my job to oversee it all
because I live closer, right?
And speaking of your dollhouse condo, which I say with all
due respect, Mum, 'cause you got it decked out so nice,
you'll be happy to know we finally made it past the Shops
on Don Mills. That's how bad the traffic is, Mum.
Plus, it's drizzling.
And by the way, Mum, sorry you have to leave the condo.
You heard that walking, talking, Spanish Inquisition of
an on-call palliative care doctor, who fancied herself some
kind of dying person's advocate. But what's the use in
protecting the dying and not the people who look after
them? The family. The caregivers. That idiot left your pain
management in my hands.
My hands!

As if I know how to administer morphine!

Oh sure, she did a lot of talking, shared lots of information, but not about you, how long you'd take and stuff. No.

It was all about her precious schedule.

Don't call between midnight and seven because doctors need their sleep, too.

Don't call nine-one-one.

And absolutely under no circumstances is it okay to take you to the hospital because the trauma of transport can kill a dying person.

Talk about a guilt trip.

Of course I nodded in agreement. You know how self-conscious I am. You know I don't think on my feet. And besides, I'm a compulsive pleaser.

I have to be when I'm not the good one, right?

Why is that Mum? Why aren't I the good one?

I'm sorry about the bumps, Mum. Construction.

And I'm sorry this is so terrible for you, but you've gotta know the driver's only going about forty. Maybe less.

And by the way, it's not as if I haven't seen people die before. Dad, Uncle Nick, Aunty Peg... shit. She died right in my arms, remember?

Don't worry, Mum. Dolores can't hear me, and, anyways, under the circumstances, I think it's okay to swear.

See Mum, the problem is I just never saw anybody so afraid to die.

Your prostrate, contorted body, your arms forward and flailing, like some kind of mummy rising from a sarcophagus. Your delirium. Your moaning. Your writhing.

It took two of us, Dolores or whatever her name is, and me just to hold you down.

You almost fell off the bed once. And don't forget you have osteo.

You said the doctor called your bones sawdust.

And that wailing? Eerie. Sorry, but it was. And the thrashing? What was that Mum?

What were you trying to do? Pin death's arms down?

I know. You can't say. I'll never hear your voice again.

We didn't know it at the time, but your last words were two days ago.

I asked you if you still wanted to do chemo, and you said, "Yes."

Do you want to hear something funny? Not funny "ha ha," but you know what I mean. Funny weird. Funny ironic.

Your chemo would have been today. Today is two days
later.
But "yes" wasn't your last word.
Your last words were after the minister held your
hand and sang your favourite hymn, *How Great Thou
Art*, and Marilyn said, "Wasn't that nice, Mum?" and you
said, and these were your exact last words, Mum, "It took
my breath away."
It took your breath away.
Remember, Mum?
Could last words be more beautiful? Luckier?
Some people yell at somebody they love or say
something awful. You know what I mean?
Shit, I'm scared.
Not that you're going to die.
I know you're going to die, Mum.
But can you wait 'til we get to Sunnybrook?
I'm just asking.
See, obviously this whole thing is my idea, and I don't want
you to die on my watch at the corner of Leslie and
York Mills, or I'll never live it down. It'll all be on me.
And anyways, it's not like I'm little anymore.
When I was little, your death was the most horrible thing I
could imagine.
I idolized you. I'd even say worshipped.
Your life mattered more than mine.
I bet you don't even know how many times I leaned on that
cold, green-speckled, granite windowsill and looked up at
the stars and cried and prayed.
Prayed, Mum.
That you'd come home safe from the party or from the
bridge game or whatever.
"Star light, star bright..."
And that David babysat us. Sorry, but that guy was a total
creep. I just never told you because you'd say I was rude.
And then you'd get home, and Marilyn would be sleeping
like her usual angelic self, and Dad would be angry because
I'd still be up. And I wouldn't even care because all that
mattered was that you were safe, and I would whisper,
"Thank you, God."
And when I was a kid, it was like living with a movie star.
Doris Day. Remember, Mum?
I thought she was beautiful, and you looked exactly like her.
And you made things fun, like when we were in the car.

You'd point out the landmarks of your life like they were
famous. Where you grew up, where you went to school,
where you nursed. And every one of those landmarks had a
story we'd hear over and over. And up until I was about
twelve, you'd ask, "What's coming up?" And Marilyn and
I would announce to the world, "There's Mummy's
hospital!" from the back seat. You loved that.
Remember?
Remember putting us to bed, you asked your little girls how
much we loved you, and we'd compete to see who loved
you more? Arms outstretched wide?
"As much as the moon and the sun."
"As much as all the sky."
"As much as every blade of grass and grain of sand."
I tried so hard to win that one.
Because you were the creator of magic in our house.
If I had a fever, you'd rub Vicks on my chest and make
Lipton's soup, and I'd be all better.
At birthdays, when other kids just got one, you'd load us up
with all the party sandwiches we wanted. We knew how to
play all the party games thanks to you. "Ring Around the
Rosie, Pin the Tail on the Donkey..."
You made sure there was always Neapolitan ice cream for
Hockey Night in Canada.
And even though you couldn't sing, you taught us songs.
"Roamin' in the Gloamin'" and "Shine on Harvest Moon" and
all the Rogers and Hammerstein musicals. And you'd make
requests when we were doing the dishes, and it made the
time go by faster 'cause I hated doing dishes.
You made us matching party dresses on the Singer from
Simplicity patterns and hard pins and bargain fabric.
You could knit the speed of light, carry on a conversation,
and figure out the killer on Perry Mason all at the same
time.
Magic.
You taught us manners, even though Marilyn seemed to be
born knowing them.
To this very day, I notice people's manners.
You taught us how to fold towels so they'd look nice in the
linen closet, and this was way before Marie Kondo.
And when I came home from Mrs. Bailey's class all
nervous and humiliated after she'd announced I got
a bad mark on the arithmetic test to the whole
goddam class, all I had to do was take in a whiff

of your spaghetti sauce and hear the words, "We're
having your favourite tonight!" and all that hurt
would vanish. Like magic.
And how to play bridge. You know it's a fad now? People
go on Mediterranean bridge cruises and stuff? Crazy, right?
How to separate an egg. Do you know I actually impressed
my friends with that in Paris?
How to set a table. How to iron. It goes on forever, Mum.
How to make hospital corners.
Well, that's not such a big deal because it was part of your
training, but you know what, Mum? It's now just hitting me
here in this ambulance. You taught us all these things,
Marilyn and me, but you came from uneducated, immigrant
parents who grew their own food and raised chickens, so
who was there to teach you? How did you learn all that
other stuff?
You were smart, Mum. That's how.
The only one in your class to finish high school.
Like I said, magic.
You know what else you gave us, Mum?
Something to look forward to. Maybe the greatest gift
of all.
Christmas? Every November the Eaton's Christmas
catalogue arrived on the doorstep. You'd set us down at the
kitchen table and say, "Santa wants you to pick out
something you'd like."
You were in cahoots with Santa! Your magic extended that
far!
And not just that, Mum. You brought us up right.
Marilyn and I would pick out something and ask if it
was too expensive.
Even though it never was. Santa could always afford it.
And all that magic you brought to your little girls, you
brought again to your grandchildren, then your great
grandchildren. That's pretty lucky, isn't it? I mean it was
horrible that you were widowed at barely fifty, and I
know in a way you never got over it. But look at the legacy
you were able to enjoy right up until a couple of days ago.
Pretty amazing.
You taught us good times are the most important thing to
have. Good people the most important thing to be. And no
matter what you might think, I am a good person, Mum. I
know I could never live up to you. Shit, people thought you
were the neighbourhood Mother Teresa for God's sake.

But I'm good, too. I am.

Even though it took me time to get here.

I don't mean here, as in Bayview. I mean to get over
myself.

You know, past disliking myself.

I know if you could right now, you'd say I always had a
chip on my shoulder.

But guess what?

I learned to be resilient. I really did.

And anyways, it wasn't about me. *You* were the one who
mattered.

You were the one who felt terrible when you were about to
give birth, and in those days, the father wasn't allowed in
the delivery room, and you made Dad promise if there was
a problem, the doctors would save you, not me because you
already had a life, and I didn't.

You were the one who felt awful up north at Ruth's cottage,
when me, a colicky baby, somehow rolled off the dock
into the lake, and you couldn't swim, but I didn't drown
because Ruth could.

You were the one who was beside yourself when I, only a
toddler, wandered from our yard to Lawrence Avenue while
you, pregnant with Marilyn, chatted with Lucy.

A car of strangers picked me up and drove me around
the neighbourhood until we found you.

I wasn't an easy kid. I get it. To this day, those stories
make up my prememory life's lore. I'm bound and
locked by your memories, as you remember them.

But can I ask you something?

Why did you have to tell me?

Telling me those stories just raised more haunting
questions to answers I'd never have.

I guess you didn't realize it, but I already thought
I was the ugliest, dumbest kid in the world and only
wanted you to love me.

I didn't think twice when I got lost in the hardware store
and in tears, ran up and down the aisles looking for you,
and when I finally found you, Mum, you hadn't even
noticed I was missing.

Or, when I was strapped down in the emerg, haemorrhaging
and hysterical, the doctor sticking those long metal tongs
down my throat and pulling out blood clots the size of
New York City roaches, and I screamed for you and later
you said the nurse wouldn't let you in.

Or when you couldn't be affectionate. I know how bad you
felt. You couldn't help it. "Cold," you called yourself. You
even apologized.
I just couldn't believe that about you. I didn't want to
believe it. Because you were my Doris Day.
"You're very affectionate, Mum!" I'd say and give you a
big hug.
Like I said, I didn't think twice.
That's the way things were.
Whatever happened, you gotta know that all I cared about
was you.
How bad or good it was for you.
When you fussed over Marilyn's hair, consumed yourself
with her health. When you said she had a better memory.
When I got a spanking every week because after seven
days, I had it coming anyway, and to be fair, sometimes
Marilyn got one too even though she never did anything wrong.
I never blamed you.
It was my fault.
I was bad.
Bad for getting into mischief and not paying attention.
Bad for being silly at the kitchen table and arguing.
Bad for saying one day at Lucy's that I wished my sister
was dead.
You washed my mouth out with soap right then and there in
front of everybody, and I knew every time your sharp nails
pricked the roof of my mouth and the bubbles seeped down
my throat that I deserved it, even though I wasn't exactly
sure what dead meant.
And how could you know I worried? Worried I was
adopted. Worried I had Down syndrome. Do you know for
years I actually studied my face in the mirror of the locked
bathroom, checking to see if my eyes were slanted, my nose
spread wide, while you were on the phone with a friend
ten feet away?
And all of this was like, life as usual, until I was a teenager
and you and Marilyn huddled together, whispering at the
kitchen table every evening, and you and I spent every
morning before school yelling at each other because maybe
I hadn't hung up a sweater or something.
And maybe I shouldn't be telling you this, but during one of
those screaming matches, you stomped off to do the laundry
and Marilyn asked me, "Why do you always make Mummy
cry?"

"Why does Mummy always make me cry?" I answered.

"And anyway, she loves you more than me."

I couldn't believe I blurted it out like that. I was ashamed of myself and hoped you didn't hear me.

It was a dare. I expected Marilyn to deny it. But you know what she said?

"I know."

She said she knew you loved her more. And when she said it, she was crying, so I knew it must be true.

How did she know that, Mum? How?

I'm sure if you could speak right now, Mum, you'd say that's crap, but she really did say it, and when she did, she validated my greatest fear. That's when I started to clue in. Clue into stuff like, you always said I reminded you of your mother. The mother who drove you nuts. Who didn't stop clinging. Who was overbearing.

Marilyn was like you, blond and mild tempered, and I was dark and hairy, just like your mother.

Just like her, a burden.

But just think about your mother, Mum, and what she came from. She was a little girl, totally impoverished, growing up in a Russian village. One morning she woke up, and her mother, your grandmother, was gone. Your mother was abandoned. Left in the care of a brutal stepfather who abused her. Starving. Working for her food. God knows what that man subjected her to. And this lasted for ten years.

Ten years, Mum, before your grandmother sent for your mother to come to Canada. And what happened when she got here? She found her mother married with a whole new family. Abandoned a second time.

Think about it. How does someone get over something like that? And it explains why your mother was so possessive. So controlling. Why she had to devour you.

She couldn't help it, Mum. None of us can.

Daughters, mothers, daughters.

We're all just links on a chain.

When you were born, you had all the attention, no siblings, and by the way, why was that? A lot of it was bad attention, but you were still the star, the darling of your step-aunts and uncles, the hero who nursed them during TB and cancer treatments to their deaths.

Only your mother didn't die. She outlived them all. She didn't stop making demands, didn't stop depending on you,

her life, a series of traumas marking your days.
Marriage was supposed to be your escape. You were
looking for freedom.
The last thing you wanted was instant motherhood.
You'd already spent your youth being a mother to your
own mother.
But barely nine months passed before I came along and
who could blame you if you thought I'd ruined things?
A screaming, shitting, puking baby?
Needy, just like your mother?
A year and half later, Marilyn was born, and her quiet
sweetness flattered your mother's ego. Marilyn made you
feel like the mother you wanted to be. Even as a baby, she
had that skill.
Later, Marilyn became the listener, the reassurer, the
comforter in your need not to be needed.
She told you what you wanted to hear. Kind of like a
surrogate mother.
Everybody needs a mother, right?
Chain reactions, like I said.
A mother abandons a daughter, that daughter suffocates
her own daughter with the love she never had, and her daughter
seeks to be a daughter to someone.
I get it, Mum. Marilyn was easier to be with. Easier to love.
That's why she grew up knowing what it felt like
to see somebody's face light up when she walked
into a room.
We're all just links in a chain, right?
It's okay because you know what? I finally learned to like
myself. See my goodness.
And you like me now too, don't you?
You see my goodness now too, don't you?
If you could, I bet you'd nod and say something like
"I always loved you both the same."
And even though I can't because it would hurt your
tender skin, I'd hug you, for sure I would.
You know, we never used to tell each other "I love you"
when I was a kid. I wanted to say it to Dad before he died,
but I was too shy. Yeah, I know. I was twenty-seven and
married at the time, but it's true.
That was another one of the wonderful things about the next
generation, your grandkids being born. Suddenly, we all
started saying, "I love you." Not "love you" like everybody
throws around these days. A real "I love you" looking right

into each other's eyes.

And even though right now you can't open your eyes, I'll say it anyways.

I love you, Mum.

You know what, Mum? You won't believe this, but I think we're here. The ambulance is pulling up to the curb.

You did it.

You made it here without dying!

Thank you, Mum.

I know you don't feel good 'cause you're wrinkling up your forehead. It is a little chilly outside even for April twenty-sixth. But don't worry. We'll be inside in a minute, and you'll be nice and warm. I promise.

Just breathe in that fresh air. Take it in deep, Mum.

Know what Mum? I just realized we should've taken a spin past the old house on our way here, but that might've been pushing our luck.

Hear that, Mum? I'm just a little teary because I'm so happy you get to hear robins before you go inside. Happy for both of us because it's a beautiful spring day.

Oops. A little bump in the walkway, but it's the only one. The rest of the ramp is smooth sailing. So, don't worry, Mum. I got you.

I got you.

All She Was and Ever Will Be

Verba volant, scripta manent.
Spoken words fly away, written words remain.
      —Latin proverb shared by Francesca

The most important thing is don't cry.
Hold it together. But how? Where do I start?
I've always been afraid to ask questions.
She once told me she'd disown a friend
who pried into her past. Will she let me
ask questions this time, or will she be as
always, her usual evasive self? Her evasive
self that was like a solid see-through wall between
us, and much as I tried, couldn't be moved or
knocked down. Her evasive self that led to a catalogue
of repeated, unanswered questions.
Like, what do I call her now?

I've always called her Francesca, though she was
more like a mother to me. Enveloping me in her care,
initiating me into her world of glorious culture
when I was alone in Paris, desperately trying to
"find myself" as we used to say, trying to escape the
problems of my youth. Then, for forty years, we
maintained our deep bond through letters and phone
calls and visits, many of them the highlights of my life.
Francesca was always there for me.
Until I found out her real name wasn't Francesca at all.
It was Jane.

"Francesca? Jane? What is your real name anyway?"

Don't sound so nervous. You're a senior for fuck's sake!

"No need for sarcasm, Kathy," Francesca says. "I've been
Francesca to you all this time. Forty years."

A bad start. Change the subject!

"I brought some sandwiches," I say.
"I always said nobody makes sandwiches like you
do," Francesca says. "What did you make us? That
fabulous salmon salad?"
"Egg salad," I say.
"My favourite!" Francesca says. "I love an egg salad
sandwich! You add just the right amount of mayonnaise
and a dash of curry, as I recall. I always told Tomas that

Therese may be French, but our Kathy's the better cook."

Our Kathy? The better cook? Wow. Does she really mean it? Therese is a pretty amazing cook. But Francesca wouldn't lie to me, would she?

"Just half, Kathy. Let's share, okay?" Francesca says. "My appetite isn't the same since Tomas died."

Food is such a great equalizer. Thank you, chickens. Thank you, eggs.

"There's some wine on the counter behind the canning jars," she says.

Wait, what? Jars? Really? Come on. That's crazy! Bringing her two-thousand-square-foot apartment across the country and squeezing it into—what is this anyway? Six hundred?

"No thanks, I'm driving."
"That's very responsible of you, Kathy," Francesca says. "Sit on one of the boxes over there where I can see you. Where does the time go? Everything is such an effort, and I'm so pudgy. I should've kept more fit. I woke up one morning and needed a walker. So much still needs to be unpacked. And my desk? Utter chaos."

Don't say it. The whole apartment is chaos, but don't say it. A year later, and it's like the day she moved in. She used to be so neat and clean. I bet there's spider webs. Daddy-longlegs. There could be roaches. Geez. If Tomas was still alive, he'd be... well, this wouldn't be happening if Tomas was still alive.

"Ten library books due, and my eyes aren't what they used to be," she says. "I can't read a book a day any more like I used to. And the mail, the newspapers! I always said if one reads *The Manchester Guardian* and *The Economist*, one is on one's way to being informed. When I pass them on, just read the highlighted sections."

What the hell! Doesn't she know how busy I am?

"I know you're busy," Francesca continues, "but think of them as conversations. Of course, it's always preferable to read in other languages too, especially the excellent *Le Monde*. I do wish *The Globe and Mail* were less biased. I'm always astonished at what the media choose to omit and how uninformed people are, so easily

brainwashed and seduced. Um... delicious, Kathy!
Every mouthful a gem. That's why I want you to read
Death in Shanghai. The author doesn't manipulate us.
Just the facts."

"You know what, Francesca?" I giggle, "I don't know why,
but for some reason this reminds me of Paris. Paris, forty
years ago, when we met. Doesn't this kind of remind
you of Paris?"

"You were adorable," Francesca smiles teasingly. "And
you haven't changed a bit."

*Adorable? Give me a break. Okay, maybe forty years
ago. But she does mean it, doesn't she? She always
made me feel so... significant.*

"Don't look like that," Francesca says. "It's true.
You wanted to knock on Simone de Beauvoir's door
and interview her, but shyness held you back. I should've
pushed you harder. I could've accompanied you to a nearby
petit café and coached you a bit. It's all about the confidence,
Kathy. While you were speaking with de Beauvoir,
I'd be on standby at a local shop or something. What
fun we would've had, discussing the whole thing after.
But you lacked the confidence, and then she died, and
it was too late. A missed opportunity. We should always
do things while we can, Kathy."

Exactly. While we can.

"Remember the first time I met you and Tomas at the
Hotel Jeanne d'Arc?" I ask. "It was actually more like
a hostel with those public toilets on every floor."

*They sure came in handy that morning I had a hangover,
puking in every single one on the way out.*

"Don't say that Kathy," Francesca says. "Jeanne d'Arc
was lovely! Le Marais, a perfect locale. Central.
Reasonable prices. Vibrant atmosphere. Anyone can stay
in the touristy areas. That was what first impressed
us about you, finding you at the Jeanne D'Arc. Natural
for responsible bohemians like Tomas and me, but you
were just a young girl with your whole life ahead of you."

*I was just a young girl trying to get away from him.
Trying not to end up dead.*

"Remember when the concierge introduced us?" I
ask. "La Canadienne, she called me?"

In truth, the last thing I wanted was to meet other tourists.
But if I had to, then Europeans at least, not other boring
Canadians. How wrong I was.

"You were a bird who'd left the nest but wasn't yet sure
how to fly," she says. "So you clung to us."
"And then, the next morning," I say, "when I found your note
under my door inviting me to lunch in your room? You
and Tomas at the table by the window? Me, sitting on your
bed because there were only two chairs? Anyway, that's what
this reminds me of."

Francesca's remembering, smiling, glowing.
It makes my heart want to burst.

"Ah, Kathy! That roast chicken!" Francesca says, "still
warm on the foil pie plate. A measly ten francs. You'd
never have found such good value in the touristy areas."
"And then the next day," I add, "you took me to the Neuilly
Marché. Tomas took that photo."
"I was wearing that smart, tan raincoat he gave me. I
still have it even though it hasn't fit in years," Francesca
says. "I just couldn't bear to throw it out."
"Yup," I nod. "Tomas always did have an eye! And
Francesca, remember those *Guide Michelin* walking
tours? Rue Du Rivoli? Boulevard St. Michel? You
made us pause and admire every statue, every plaque, every
post and fixture. You didn't miss a thing."

Other tourists actually stared at us. Francesca was loud with
that awful accent. I made fun of it, until I got sucked
into the magnificent aura of excitement she created.

"I always said enthusiastic people like us find each
other," Francesca says.
"And remember the artists' café with the opera-singing
owner?" I ask.
"M Duquesne," Francesca nods. "Tomas and I were the only
non-Parisians who knew about him."

Here comes the inevitable Arctic...

"I always said if I was in the Arctic in a room with
a hundred people, I'd find the most interesting one to
talk to," Francesca says.

Now the roses...

"I always said God gave us memories so we'd
have roses in December," she sighs.

A perfect segue. Go for it!

"You know," I say, "I've never told you this before, but
I really missed you when you left Paris."
"I know," Francesca says. "That's why when we got to
Amsterdam, I started my tradition of writing you every
Christmas Day so you'd know I was thinking of you."
"I felt sort of... actually... very... alone," I say.

You were a lost cause, a casualty.

"But you had such bravado," Francesca says.

Ready to jump seven stories from your Juliette balcony.

"Then I got that au pair job, like you suggested."

What would've happened if she hadn't come along?

"All I did was encourage you," Francesca says.

It was so much more. She saw something in me.
Francesca made me see something in me.

"And it's thanks to you I went to Alliance Française,"
I say, "and after that, everything fell into place."

It wasn't as if I oozed "broken" or something on the
outside, but he'd left my insides a mess of shattered shards.
Somehow, in one short week, abracadabra, please and
thank you, Francesca picked up those shards and handed them
back to me whole. I looked at myself in the glass and
for the first time, I liked what I saw. Nobody knew me in
Paris. I could start again. Reinvent myself. Be anything
I wanted. And for a whole, precious year that's what I did.
I lived in the enchanted Quartier Latin. I worked for the
family of a well-known playwright. I shared the seventh
floor servants' quarters with other au pair girls from
faraway countries.
I studied French. I tutored English to suave businessmen
in cozy cafes for extra francs and spent those francs
on the night train talking to Italian soldiers and discovering
on my days off, the miracle of Europe. I had midnight
dinners with intellectuals and afterwards, shared
Gauloises in the courtyard with tiny, arthritic Mme
Quesnell, the concierge, when she caught me sneaking

past her window.
I had a love affair with a handsome Frenchman who
thought my accent was exotic. He took me to his
mountain chateau where goats roamed freely. My
troubled past became a blur. I was loveable after all.
All was no longer lost. I had the promise of tomorrow
in my heart. My life's course changed. And it all
happened after I met Francesca. It was all because of
Francesca. She saved me, and I loved her for it.

"You did it all on your own, Kathy,"
Francesca says.
"But it was thanks to you. You convinced me."
"You'd already done that just by leaving him, going to Paris,"
she says. "Give yourself more credit. I told you,
first love is a madness. A madness, Kathy. It blinds
us and destroys us."
"Francesca," I say, "what about your first love?"
"First loves are all the same," Francesca says.

There she goes, stonewalling me, only this time
I'm on to her. Go ahead. Ask her about those letters.
Was her first love the one who began every letter
with "My dear Jane" and signed, "Love Burt?"
Or was hers Henry, the guy who claimed to be the only
one who really loved her? Was it so wrong to read
those letters? Or did she save them on purpose so I would?
Ask her before it's too late!

"Can you tell me about your past?" I ask.
"One can regret stirring up the past. True, memory is
a strong force," Francesca says, "but when thoughts
of yesterday creep into the mind, it's best to train
ourselves not to dwell on them."

There she goes, messing with me again. Cagey. Cryptic.
Then she sweeps me off my feet with her words.

"But for me," I say, "your past was like, well, your life
started in Paris in seventy-five when we met."
"In a way, it did. Tomas and I were together less than a
decade. Our happy days were not yet over. With time, I
told you everything."

Everything? Come on! Then who is that strange woman
and little boy Tomas is sitting with in the photo taken
in Budapest before he met you?

89

"You know Kathy? I always said if I were giving
marriage courses, I'd tell young women not to be so
agreeable," Francesca says. "The sad fact is that
women still don't realize they have choices. And
time apart. Time apart should be written right into
the marriage contract. A lot of marriages fail simply
because people get on each other's nerves. The irony
is with Tomas gone, that's all I have now is time alone."

Her sadness is too painful. Console her.

"You two had a wonderful life together," I say.
"During the early years," she says. "Tomas was so
interesting and that marvelous Hungarian black humour!
Of course, the problem with European men—other than
Italians, and I always said you must set up your daughter
with a nice Italian man—is that they aren't interested in
improving the house. I had to fight with Tomas for everything,
even getting the carpets professionally cleaned.
He loved bike riding yet wouldn't weed the terrace
plants. But that's a way of keeping fit, too."
"Most men don't like doing housework," I say.
"Don't stick up for him, Kathy," Francesca says.
"Tomas was lazy, and I had to do everything. Clean
up after him, dispose of his empty wine bottle.
The only time he carried dishes to the sink was
when we had company. But don't you dare think
he was showing off. He just wanted to get the ball
rolling and end the evening. He could be charming
for short periods, but eventually he became grumpy.
I should've established ground rules, like you did
in your marriage, but I didn't want to make a fuss."

Ground rules? Where does she get this stuff?
Anyway, let her ramble. Just listening to her mind
at work makes me feel good.

"I've always preferred smooth, harmonious relationships,
but alas," Francesca says, "Tomas was
never able to eliminate the wounded, disappointed
child inside. As he aged, it suited him to be a fatalist.
What a copout. For all his genius, he should've moved
up the job ladder, but his expertise was never appreciated."
"You two shared so much... opera, architecture," I say.
"I always said we'd walk ten miles to see a well-built
bridge," Francesca says. "The problem was Tomas

didn't practise self-examination, and helping him led
to disastrous results, even when my purpose was his
intellectual stimulation."

I wasn't just grateful for her suggestions. I lived for them.
She gave me everything and asked nothing in return.
Now I understand that asking nothing was the one
tragic flaw in our relationship.

"I always said Hungarian husbands are dark," she says.
"When I meet a woman married to a Hungarian, I
immediately pass on my condolences. They think
childless couples are best and, at most, one child
per family. A two-child family is a catastrophe."

Is she trying to tell me the woman in the photo is
Tomas's first wife? The boy his son? Francesca once
said she had wanted children, but Tomas didn't. Was it
because he already had one child? The Hungarian quota?
Is that why they travelled back and forth to Hungary all those
years?
To see his son?

"With age, Tomas became more imperious,"
Francesca says. "Expecting me to be perfect,
complaining bitterly about my cooking. Nothing
was ever good enough. I'm so happy you don't
have marital strife."

How can she be so presumptuous, and why do I
always let her get away with it? Geez!

"A great impertinence," Francesca continues, "even
if it was due to Tomas's own self-dissatisfaction. He
couldn't stop nagging me, and it's not as if I did anything
seriously wrong like leave the butter out all night."

She's doing that thing. Following my reaction in
her periphery but pretending she isn't. Don't smile!
She'll think I'm laughing at her even though it's just
a nervous reaction.

"It's devastating when a man of Tomas's calibre can't
give more direction to his life," Francesca says.
"But Tomas always put you first," I say. "You always
had the best quality coat."

Idiot! Why did I say that? As if coats matter!

91

"He didn't trust me to shop for myself!" Francesca
says. "And he had nothing else to do."
"Nobody was more loyal," I say.
"Loyal but insular," Francesca says. "And proud
of it. When he wanted to communicate with the
world, he would let us know."

*Francesca looks so feeble right now, sitting there in her
bathrobe, eating her sandwich, too angry to admit
how much she misses Tomas. Maybe she's in pain
from the cancer? God, her nails are dirty. Her eyes
are probably worse from the diabetes. I should've
made sure she washed her hands.*

"Whereas I am always stimulated by good conversation,"
she continues without skipping a beat. "I prayed for
the gift of time to get on with my interests, but Tomas
preferred to be bossy. His insufferable arrogance in
our language classes never allowed him to be incorrect.
If only he'd had his own life and let me have mine."

*And still, no matter what, she manages to muster
energy, strength.
How I wish I could be like her. Be her.*

"When people retire, they..." I stumble.
"Listen," Francesca says. "Even when Tomas had
work, he didn't understand the art of compromise.
He couldn't handle things. His lordship used up all
the little discipline he had for his work colleagues.
Anger tears at the very fabric of a marriage, Kathy."
"But," I say, "Tomas had integrity. I mean, he wasn't a
womanizer or a gambler or something."
"Must there always be something!" she demands.

I'm such a loser. Stop trying so hard!

"There are lots of civilized, courteous men who are
not drinkers or gamblers," Francesca says. "Although
all men are on some sort of power trip, I suppose.
Kurt, for example. I do admire him, but he never lets
his wife finish a story if he feels she's talked long
enough. As you once said, Kathy, 'men are such
gods.' I've always loved that turn of phrase."
"Remember Tomas called you 'goosie?'" I ask. "He ensured
you never had to earn a pay cheque. You were free."
"I certainly was not free!" Francesca says. "I wish I'd
worked. I should've. Sometimes we survived on

apples and turnips just to serve guests sparkling wine
and goulash with Tomas's home-made pasta and my
shortcakes with fresh strawberries and crème fraiche."

How could I ever forget Francesca and her famous dinner
parties! The guests treated like royalty. Me treated like
royalty...

"You know Kathy," Francesca says, "guests think
their obligation is complete if they bring a bottle,
but hospitality is time consuming. There's the
planning, the shopping, the cleaning, the cooking."
"I know," I say, "but you were sort of free, weren't you?
You travelled. Asia, Europe... Anyway, things never
got so bad you had to leave him or anything."
"How do you know!" Francesca says, her eyes
filling up. "I packed my bags more than once. Life
is too precious. You shouldn't pry, Kathy. It only
leads to hurtful results."

Shit. Houston, we have a problem.

"Sorry," I say, fighting back a pout.
"I only came home because I was so responsible," Francesca
stammers. "Don't you see? Ethics and good manners
are ingrained in me."

Somehow, I have to recover from this. Get her to smile.

"Speaking of good manners," I say, "how about
some tea?"
"Lovely," Francesca says. "A hot cup of tea is a
wonderful afternoon pick-me-up. And another
of those fabulous egg salad sandwiches. You're
such a treasure, Kathy. Did I tell you I saw two
fine films this week on the excellent Turner Classic Movies?"

Here she goes, changing the subject. Pure sabotage.

"I've never been a great fan of American cinema,"
she says, "but once in a while Hollywood does it
right. *My Fellow Americans*, a delightful spoof
with Jack Lemmon—now he had integrity—and
An Unmarried Woman with Jill Clayburgh.
Remember her? A good 'B' film. The feminists
loved it because it confirmed their opinion about
men, but I loved it because Clayburgh was fortunate
in the end to be young, attractive, have that nice
daughter and that lovely Manhattan apartment.

Most women would settle for half as much."
"Yeah, the acting was good," I say.
"*Beaches* is another one," Francesca continues. "A
good 'B' film without the traditional happy ending.
And that Bette was wonderful as the needy
character. We've all known women like her.
Demanding constant attention. Like that Therese."

This is my "in." Go for it!

"You know, Francesca," I say, "sometimes Therese tells
me stuff. Stuff about you. I just want you to know
I never pry. I guess she just thinks I need to know."
"The need to know is a selfish one, Kathy," Francesca
says. "Therese always needs to know."
"But shouldn't people know each other equally?" I
ask. "You knew everything about me from the beginning."
"You always confided in me openly," Francesca responds,
"But I didn't ask you to."

In other words, I'm a sucker as usual.

"Discretion is the better part of valour," Francesca
says. "People tell me personal details all the time.
Take Heather. Some man asked her out on a date,
and she was so excited! But after the date, she never
mentioned him again, and it was awkward. I didn't know
what to say and wished she hadn't told me. Now there's
a great short story for you, Kathy. I give it to you."

Dammit! It's not Heather I need to know about!

"I trusted you, Francesca," I say. "And now I feel like,
well, you didn't trust me back."
"Don't say that, Kathy. Of course, I trust you,"
she says.
"You wouldn't even tell me your birthday."
"I was happy to tell you my birthday," Francesca
says. "I didn't choose to share the year I was born."
"See? That's what I mean," I say. "Then Therese blurts
it out one day. 1932."
"Therese digs and digs," Francesca says. "The
first thing she asks someone is their age, and she's
offended if they don't want to tell."
"I told Therese not to tell me your age," I say. "I told
her you're super private!"

*At the time, I was foolish enough to think discovering
Francesca's real age was a breakthrough. I had no idea
how pathetically little I knew about her.
I didn't even know what I didn't know.*

"Thank you, Kathy," Francesca says. "I always
said of all my friends that you have the most empathy.
It's one of the things I love about you."

*She loves me? She loves me! She's never actually
said it before. Then why after all these years does
she keep secrets from me? Aren't secrets like Christmas
cards? Meant to be exchanged?*

"You see, Kathy," Francesca says, "For all her
brilliance, Therese has a small mind. She really
does distress me. Counting the rice kernels in each
piece of sushi? Endlessly reusing plastic garbage bags?
Truly worthy of SCTV. When the psychiatrist said she
could stop coming, she kept going anyway."
"Why?" I ask.
"Because as Tomas said, it was covered under OHIP!"
Francesca laughs. "Therese can't resist a bargain.
Always has to be centerstage. Everything's a discussion.
Needy, like the Bette character. Therese never got over
being adopted. For years, I was a crutch to needy
friends who believed I had nothing but time on my hands."

*Maybe we're all needy. But the truth is we're drawn
to Francesca and just love to be with her.*

"Therese was no exception," Francesca says. "I see
how she feeds off people. And scandal! Just takes
a scenario and runs with it. I made the mistake of
introducing her to Ian, and she couldn't wait to
inform me that he is 'like so.' That's what we
called it in my day. As if I didn't already know!
At least with Ian, I always learn something."

*I left every conversation with her feeling I'd learned
something. But what could she learn from me?*

"Therese means well though," I say.
"I'm not so sure, Kathy," Francesca says. "She's
jealous, suspicious. She asked me if Samuel had
ever gotten fresh with me!"

*Samuel? Therese's husband? He's got to be at least
twenty years younger than Francesca.*

"Are you serious?"

"I could never be with anyone as frugal as Samuel,"
Francesca says. "Men in general are such a
nuisance. One is enough. Since Tomas died,
Therese has pried about our sex life, pestered me
why the funeral wasn't Catholic. Honestly!"

*Tomas was Catholic? Tomas was Catholic! I knew
that but somehow it didn't register. Maybe Tomas
couldn't divorce his first wife? Maybe Tomas and
Francesca were "living in sin" as we used to say?
Maybe that's why they told different stories about how
they met? Why the location of their wedding always
changed? Maybe that big fucking story about losing
her wedding ring was made up? Why they never had
kids? A thousand things could be answered by that
one detail alone. Only I don't know the detail. Somehow
I've got to get the detail. But don't, no matter what,
don't sound desperate, or she'll shut right down.
Just act casual, as if the detail doesn't matter.*

"Are you kidding me?"

"I'm telling you" Francesca says. "She knows no
boundaries, that Therese, but don't you waste your
energy on her. Try to discipline yourself not to allow
your worries to control you. Promise me you'll teach
your daughter that."

*Sure! No problem! My adult daughter is all ears.
People without children are always the big child
experts.*

"But getting back to what we were saying." I say,
"Sometimes I don't feel like I really know you."

"Of course you do, Kathy," Francesca says.

*No, I didn't. No, I don't. Tell her. I have to
tell her. Just say it.*

"I thought all this time you were an orphan."

"I may as well have been," she says.

*Like firing bullets, those quips. How does she do that
unless she can read my mind?*

"Then Therese tells me you went to your mother's
funeral," I say. "Your mother's been alive all these years,
and you never let on. Never even mentioned her."

"Vi was horrible and a terrible mother," she says.

"But I don't get it," I say.

"She was fifteen and had no business giving birth," Francesca says. "She married some policeman by lying about her age, and her father had the marriage annulled."

Oh God. Oh my God. Is that it? Was Francesca born out of wedlock? Illegitimate, they used to call it?

"And you and your mother lived in Montreal?"

"At first," Francesca says. "Then when I was five, Vi sent me to live in Toronto."

"You had family here?" I ask.

"They were Vi's friends," she says.

Wait, what? Her mother sent her away? To friends? In another province? An innocent child?

"They must have been really close friends," I say.

"Not really," Francesca says. "Vi paid them, and they gave me a good home."

Don't show pity and embarrass her.

"So, Toronto was like a second home?"

"You could say so," Francesca says. "Anyway that's the kind of thing Vi did. Whatever was best for her."

How can she say it so calmly? So matter-of-factly? Having been passed around like a... like a thing?

"But eventually you returned to Montreal?"

"As a teenager, when Vi got married," Francesca says.

She never had a mother. She never had a child. How did she know how to be a mother to me?

"Vi's hubby was a good man, but he did her bidding," Francesca continues. "Hopped to her like a tin soldier. All I cared about were my teachers, the nuns. Talk about devotion. They gave up their lives for us. Everything I know is thanks to the nuns."

"But what about your real father?" I ask. "Did you ever meet him?"

"Only once," Francesca says, "after I'd left home for good. I wasn't impressed. Apparently, he drank."

"What do you mean 'left for good?'"

"I was eighteen," she says. "After that, I didn't see Vi again until... until her funeral. That's why I never bothered to mention her, Kathy."

"But I still don't get it."

"Vi and I had a fight. A terrible fight," she says. "I got
fed up and left."

Is it true, or is it her truth? Is she saving face
because her mother Vi dumped her twice?

"But sorry, Francesca, it doesn't make sense," I say.
"You're not a fighter, you're a... a discusser."

"I baked a cake, and Vi said I put in too much
sugar, so I packed my bags and left," Francesca says.

A home falls apart because of too much sugar? But it's
clear. She expects me to believe it, demands I believe it.

"But what about your sister?" I ask. "Therese says you
have a sister."

"Half-sister," she says.

"Well, what's she like?"

"I never knew her," Francesca says. "I left just
after she was born. Since Vi's funeral, I see she's
very nice. Religious. Listen, Kathy, it's not as if
I misled you, you know. You once called me in
a panic because someone upset you."

Once? I turned to Francesca every time I was in
pain. I cried in her face. I turned to her every time
I was happy. She was happy for me. She was my
life's sounding board.

"As I told you at the time," Francesca continues,
"ignoring things is generally a good way to get
through life. Although it's not to be confused with
your parents ignoring your marriage to a good man.
That was incorrect. The point is it's best to develop a
thick skin in life. If you do feel hurt now, I never
intended it. I always said if I ever had a daughter,
I'd want her to be exactly like you, Kathy."

"Thank you," I say.

What else can I say when she says stuff like that?

"I always said you were the daughter I always
wanted," she says.

Good to know I'm the daughter somebody wanted.

"And you're the mother I always wanted," I say.

She's smiling again.

"Your mother means well," Francesca says. "But
she doesn't always appreciate you. You have so much
to give. You are one of life's great givers. Every
Christmas, every birthday we were astounded by your
generosity."

*Meanwhile, she complained about the books because
she'd already read them.*

"You and Tomas were always so special to me," I say.

*It's a quiet moment full of love. Is she feeling it too?
If only she would look me in the eye.*

"By the way, did you ever read *The Tamarind Seed?*"
Francesca asks. "What about *The Walnut Tree?*"
I always said I'm never bored so long as I have
access to the public library, Sunday afternoon
opera, *Al Jazeera,* and of course the marvellous
Masterpiece Theatre. Did I mention that wonderful
Thomas Hardy piece? There was a fascinating
doc on St. Laurent. People are so unsophisticated,
Kathy. Delicate hot house plants. But you and I
lead rich, full lives because we don't depend on
others to entertain us."

*No, no, no! She's coming around the club house turn.
She's getting tired. Think of something!*

"Hey Francesca, remember when I came home from
Paris, you two lived on Gerrard?"

*I thought the building was pretentious because I'd
never seen security before. But as usual, they were
ahead of their time. What an idiot I was!*

"We just loved that nobody could simply drop
in unexpectedly," she says. "People with lots
of time on their hands understand an appointment
but not if I'm busy reading. How I loved the access
to Toronto cuisine! La Croissanterie, those splendid
Shopsy's smoked meat sandwiches. I never thought
I'd find a good deli after I left Montreal. And culture!
Tarragon pay-what-you-can matinees. One never
needed money to enjoy Toronto's best offerings."

*I was laughing my ass off the time she showed up
to the concert in slippers because of swollen feet.
But she held her head high, and my friends swooned.*

"Shaw and Stratford close by," she continues, "the
free lectures. I once attended an Irving Layton poetry
reading, and he, by the way, was a magnificent-looking
man, and I thought how fascinating he was, shocking
his audience like he did. Toronto was heaven. But we
drained our savings and had to move out west where
Tomas could find work."

In some ways, our best years were from a distance.
The phone calls, the visits, but, best of all, the letters.
Me, in my Toronto kitchen on a lawn chair at a
card table, tapping away on a typewriter about
motherhood and mortgage payments.
She, stuck out west, writing glorious letters,
which really were accounts, reflections,
testimonials, histories that could've, should've been
published. Reading her letters, I always felt I was
missing out on some crucial life experience just by
not being in her presence. Those letters were a lonely,
young mother's lifeline.
Thank God, I still have them.

"We kept in touch by letter," I say, "But
now it seems as if I only wrote about my silly life,
while you..."
"Your letters were beautifully written, Kathy,"
Francesca says. "I cherished them. Your
métier was writing about family and friends. Do
write about your Paris love one day. You could
start with something like, "I swear I saw him on
the street today, but how can that be when he killed
himself years ago?" Or you could do murder mysteries.
Write about your hysterical Jewish family and
throw a murder in, a vendetta, or something. I
always wished I lived nearby when your children
were little so I could rush over and give you
hours to write. You must write naturally, in the
now. You don't express yourself as well in the
past. I loved what you wrote about marriage..."

Didn't she say marriage was overrated? Didn't
she say women gave up their independence?

"...and motherhood," she continues. "I was so
proud when you got that newspaper column on
parenting. How did you do it? Raising a family
and teaching full time and writing that column?"

She's proud of me. Now that I think about it, how
did I do it? I actually did. It feels good now to have
done it. Nobody else even noticed. God, she makes
me feel important. She's always has. As if I matter.
That's how she switches the tables, takes the focus off
herself. That's why she knows everything about me and
I know so little about her.
If this was a hockey game, she just scored in
overtime.

"I guess I had a lot of energy in those days," I say.
"I always said you must write a book of essays,"
Francesca says. "Of course, you'll have to change the names."

Does she have any idea how crazy that sounds?
Change the names? Like she did in her own, real
life? Shrouding herself in mystery? Lying to me
even as I poured my heart out to her?
I only discovered Francesca's real name at her
funeral. It was on the passport her sister
showed me. She was Jane to her sister.
Francesca to me. A life split, divided.
Two parts of a whole unaware of each other. But why?
Why?
Her sister knew even less of her than I did. Together,
we tried to assemble the puzzle, but there
were too many missing pieces.
All we could do was kneel side by side over
Francesca's stillness in the coffin and say a prayer
for all she was, all she'll ever be.
To her sister, the sibling she never knew.
To me, the woman who came into my life as a
tourist and left it as a mother.
All of those unanswered questions, and now it's
too late. She's gone. All her stories, her life, gone.
She died without trusting anyone, not even me.
A missed opportunity.
Yet, despite all the unanswered questions, despite
her dishonesty, despite her distrust, despite never
knowing the woman I saw as a mother, it was worth
it. More than worth it.
Because I may never know what she really thought,
what she really felt or even who she really was.
But I do know one thing.
I know how I felt.
Loved.

So, I won't cry. Instead, just like Francesca would,
I will choose to be grateful.
I'll look at her portrait. The one she left to me.
Not Therese or anyone else. Me.
I'll keep talking to it. Keep listening to it. When I'm
hurt, I'll hear her consoling voice.
I'll look into her haunting, crystal-blue eyes and even
if that wall of evasiveness rises again, I won't give up.
I'll keep asking the questions.
Again and again and again.

6. Ellen O'Donnell Walters

Ellen has enjoyed writing since starting a diary as a young child. She has continued to write poetry and short stories throughout her varied career as an educator in the roles of teacher, special education consultant, school principal, leadership development administrator, and instructor for aspiring teachers and principals. A driving force of hers has been ensuring supports, which can be life changing, for students facing learning challenges. She is grateful for each day of retirement and the time to craft stories, which, like a good education, can be a lasting legacy to her children, granddaughter, and her widening family circle.

The Routine

Every night
alone in the battered kitchenette
the lights dimmed
the children dented and banned to bed
her husband out in the somewhere
throwing his daily grind down a slot machine
or on some seductive table with such damp fury
that their lives would be forever circumscribed
·   by this tiny, rented space.

Every night
she scrubs down the patch of floor,
swabs off gobs of dismay
and the odd splotches of rage so that
every morning blushing with hope
a spotless smoothness
will greet her ragged soul,
as she lights her first cigarette,
ready to incinerate another day.

Island Mother

We made it to the Island with our mother in the summer of 1953. The place Torontonians call "the Island" actually was once a peninsula. A muscular storm swept the land connection away a century before, leaving a scattered jigsaw of fifteen variously named, shaped, and sized islands rimmed with multiple beaches, boardwalks, and bridges, facing every direction on the compass. Disoriented Island visitors can get their bearings by the sight of Toronto's sprouting buildings across the harbour.

That day, my brother Tommy, nearly two, and I, aged four, were disoriented too. As the ferry from the city nudged the Ward's Island dock, we knew only one thing about the Island: It meant no more home.

And as we were soon to learn, it also meant a whole lot worse.

My mother Shirley hurried us along the dock. I didn't know why we were there. It would have been hard for her to explain, and she had other things on her mind. After the most recent beating by my father, she had been hospitalized. She had suggested that maybe Tommy was not his son. In the 1950s world, wife-beating jokes peppered everyday banter. Police routinely viewed complaints as husband and wife problems to be sorted out between them. One doctor advised my mother to just learn to cook better. Women's shelters hadn't been invented.

And her parents were not going to help. Shirley's divorced mother drowned each day in cheerful delirium with her first love—alcohol. Her father and his new wife nursed a bruising estrangement from Shirley.

So she was on her own to deal with our father, Francis, who was just beginning to establish himself as a lawyer. Her waitressing helped support him through law school. He was now a man who could navigate the legal system, which at the time deemed only adultery to be grounds for a divorce.

But she had a getaway plan. She was the sole owner of the tiny Toronto bungalow where we had lived for the past few years. Without Francis's knowledge, she sold it to her brother for one dollar. That day, once Francis had left for work, she gave the all-clear to a moving van to back up to the bungalow. That evening, Francis opened the front door to echoing rooms, empty except for a pile of his clothes and his toothbrush on top. There was no toothpaste. And no family.

She had rented the island cabin for the summer. She was drawn to islands. Perhaps she was soothed by the solitude and watery distance from trouble. I didn't know where we'd be going after the summer. Maybe she didn't know either.

On the island, time for me flowed into itself marked by events that were disparate dramas in a sea of things forgotten. The geography of our new universe was the cabin—plank floors, walls, ceiling, a dry kitchen, and off it, a porch bedroom for our mother and an alcove filled by Tommy's crib and my cot. Outside, the world was of slim trees trying to stay upright in sand and a path that rolled towards the endless lapping lake. Alongside the path was an outdoor water tap, shared with other cabins.

Also shared with other cabins was the outhouse. When we arrived, my mother brought me inside. Daylight seeping through seams in the wood walls revealed the high bench with its menacing hole. Terrified, I was enveloped by the wet reek from the darkness below. I gripped the bench with both hands, so not to fall in. Above me an enormous spider dangled from an edifice of web and insect corpses, waiting I thought, to jump on me.

That night people from nearby cabins made a bonfire. My mother sat me on the ground to watch and told me that she had to go talk to someone. Her thin silhouette disappeared among the black saplings. The cabin people gathered around the fire, laughed, and passed bottles of drinks while one man strummed a guitar to scattered singing. I didn't know the songs. No one looked my way as I sat at the fringe, searching faces for someone who knew me. The chill of disconnection settled into me.

And I really had to pee. Mother wasn't anywhere I could see. I held on. And held on. My eyes tracked each person who came out of the ghastly outhouse. They looked unconcerned by whatever had gone on inside. I could hold on no more. I had to do it. I flew over the cold ground, up the step and pushed in the door. The inside was a black shock, unlike my daytime visits. I clambered onto the horrible bench, gripped the edge, and let fly. The spider was surely somewhere in pursuit. I leaped down and out into the night.

It was just the three of us in the cabin, at least at first. We could have been there weeks or months before a man appeared in the doorway. It was jarring. He was tall, with a leather jacket over shoulders that seemed wide as a wall and filled the entranceway. His eyes, the colour of metal, took us and the room in, as he and my mother began to talk. Their voices were quiet. Then he walked around, inspecting the cabin. The floorboards shifted under my feet.

Sometime that summer, my mother began to stay in her bed during the day. She didn't move much. I didn't know what was wrong. Fifty years later, I would be sent her journals and medical records by relatives I was able to find—documents which offered possible clues. On the island, she may have been ambushed by symptoms that had pounced from time to time since her early teens: blurred vision, deafness, numbness, a loss of balance, and a looming sense of terror. These overtook her from time to time but then would fade. Doctors proposed different diagnoses. Psychiatry was tried. Near the end of the war, she was discharged from the Royal Canadian Navy, where she had been a telegraph operator intercepting enemy messages. Deemed to be medically unfit for service, she was admitted to the Toronto veterans' hospital. But it would take another forty years, and towards the end of her life, before she would be diagnosed with relapsing-remitting multiple sclerosis. Its capricious flares and retreats by then had become a sustained attack.

From her bed in our cabin, she talked to me about doing some things myself. I decided to get her tea, which I knew she liked. But how to do this?

I filled a kitchen teacup from the outdoor tap and mixed in some dirt to make it the right dark tea colour. This took some careful mixing. I balanced the cup on a saucer like a grownup and staggered across the lumpy ground. Her tea was sloshing out. In a fury, I hurled the saucer to the sand. With both hands in an angry tightness around the cup, I trudged on. My mother said she liked her tea. But Tommy stood straight as a little stick in his crib, crying and soggy looking. There was a smell coming from his crib. I didn't know what to do about that.

On another day, the tall man was back. He strode past me and stood in her bedroom doorway. Behind him, my mother's voice came from the bed. His metal eyes looked at me as if considering what to do about a piece of furniture. The aloneness that settled in me at the strangers' bonfire welled up. Something about this man told me to go outside, so I did.

That day presented additional problems. Someone was in the outhouse for a long, long time and while waiting, I had wet my pants—not for the first time. In fact, all my three or four pairs of underpants needed cleaning. How to do this? I decided to wash them in the lake and slogged along the squishy sand path to the beach, my wet underwear itching and the skin of my legs burning. The cool, murky lake water played around me as I sat waist deep in a state of blissful relief.

Next, I began swishing and squeezing the several other pairs of underwear. The more I swished them in the water, the dirtier they looked. I swished them again. They got browner and browner. I didn't know that the silty muck that had been accumulating for thousands of years to create the islands was also accumulating on my undies. Defeated and frustrated to tears, I hung them to dry, saggy and streaked, on the branches of a driftwood log jutting from the sand.

By then, hunger howled inside me. I became a food-finding entity. I and the seagulls knew that visitors left partially finished food, such as hot dog buns or bags of snacks, around in the sand. Sometimes they put leftovers in the battered oilcan near the log. I climbed up on the log and peered inside the oil can but could not decipher or reach whatever was deep down in there.

Two teenagers were sunbathing on towels and had been watching as I tried to wash my underwear in the lake. They offered me something to eat—half a bag of Cheesies. I devoured the salty orange sticks and could not help looking around to see if there was anymore. They asked where I lived. I waved towards the path with orange fingers. One girl walked with me in that direction, and we scanned each one of the identical cabins lined up along pathways. They all belonged to other people. A panic charged through me. What if we never could find where I lived? And then the outhouse appeared and just beyond, our cabin.

Back in the city, my father was also having problems. His home gone, he moved into his law office, sleeping on the anteroom couch. He had slept in much worse conditions during the war, fighting through Sicily, Italy, Belgium, and Holland as a teen in the Canadian infantry. For some time after coming home to his parents' house, he would not use a bed and continued to sleep fully dressed on the floor, attack ready. Or escape ready. Domestic battles raged with his parents.

But now telling them that his wife and the kids had disappeared was harder than all that had preceded. At first, there was shocked shouting from his mother and from his father, worse—a silent, folded-arm fury. Their Catholicism held that marriage was sacred and insoluble; divorce was never a consideration. And their grandchildren had to be found. When the uproar wore itself down, his mother produced a pot of tea, and they formulated a plan. The marriage would be put back together by taking us from Shirley so that she would be forced to return to Francis in order to have her children. But first we had to be found. Above all, this marriage catastrophe was to be kept within the family as much as possible and without involvement of authorities.

The rolling catastrophe of Shirley and Francis's marriage had begun as a grand rail adventure across Canada. Their postwar elopement at age twenty-one and twenty-two, respectively, and honeymoon on Vancouver Island was as far away from Toronto and their parents as they could get. While they were on that distant island, Shirley later wrote, she felt "almost safe."

But five years later, hiding on Ward's Island, she was down to one hundred pounds.

My father hired a detective to find us. Wes was also a veteran. His assignments and skills during the war equipped him to find people. But Wes's army record was blighted by at least one crime committed during the war. While he was stationed in Aldershot, England, he murdered a prostitute. His military lawyer at the pre-court martial hearing argued that since Wes had incurred multiple shrapnel injuries, predicted to be fatal, he likely wouldn't live long after a trial. He was demoted and docked pay, sidestepping further punishment. My father, years later, described Wes as a "crazy man with a steel plate in his head."

Wes was the man with the metal eyes standing in front of my mother's bedroom door.

At some point, Wes informed my father of our whereabouts. My father and his parents selected a team of three to get us from the island, consisting of a legal parent, an additional male back up in case of a fight, and a female as a caregiver. The regular island ferry would not be used. In a water taxi hired for a round trip were a cousin by marriage, Sergeant Charles Rebbeck in his immaculate Canadian Army uniform, my father hunched in his overcoat, and his young sister Catherine, her face grave and frightened. She brought two blankets. The weather was getting cooler.

My mother stood in her bedroom doorway when the three entered our cabin. Francis spoke to her in a tight voice, and she made a short remark, turning her face away. I heard nothing more, as blankets descended on us.

Tommy was picked up by our Aunt Catherine, and I was lifted off my feet by Charles Rebbeck, who smelled of fresh soap. Seeing our island world now from high off the ground, we were out the cabin door, floating over the sandy path to the dock, and set down deep into the water taxi. Years later my mother wrote that she "gave up the children," and in the same letter, she added that we were "abducted".

That day was many things.

Our Aunt would later describe us as being in very poor shape, as Tommy had the distended stomach of a malnourished child. The boat veered away from Ward's Island and across the harbour. Although I couldn't see much over the sides, the city was expanding before us. Once we landed, I watched our father, his voice menacing, argue with a cab driver who refused to let Tommy and me in his vehicle due to our dirty condition. The taxi driver shouted back and would not unlock his car doors.

Another car appeared, and we were put inside without comment. I don't know who that was. It was a silent ride.

The oak door at our grandparents' opened. Inside were people who seemed to know us well, but I wasn't yet sure how I knew them. Next there was a bath in the high sided white tub, followed by tea, and buttered toast cut in finger length strips, covered with cinnamon and sugar.

We were never to see our mother again.

Whatever the unheard words were that passed between our parents that day, it would not have been about putting their marriage back together. By that fall, she was pregnant with Wes's child. Wes wanted to have only her but not take on a toddler and preschooler. And as she later wrote, she saw Wes as the only one who would rescue her.

I later learned that about four years after our island stay, my mother, by then divorced from Francis and married to Wes, came back to live in Toronto. This time she was hiding from Wes, who, after an escalating series of threatening incidents, had just tried to kill her. He held her down on a kitchen chair and ordered her to choose and drink down one of two glasses of indistinguishable clear liquids he had placed on the table. Choose and drink, or else. One glass contained vodka and the other, ethylene glycol. The latter choice, she realized, would look like a suicide. She reached out, knocked both glasses over and escaped, leaving three-year-old Mary forever behind with Wes. After several years, she relocated to Vancouver Island with a new partner and their baby daughter, Lisa. Shirley continued to live on that island in terror that Wes, who was very good at finding people, would do so.

Ellen and Tommy a Year Later

My father continued to live out of his office. After a few visits, he ended all contact with us and his family.

We grew up in a world on the other side of that solid oak door, under the care of our grandparents and aunts.

The island is now largely parkland complete with children's rides, paddle boats shaped like swans, as well as restaurants and concession stands, where Cheesies are sometimes available. The cabins and residences were bulldozed to make way for public parks, with the exception of a small community of leased homes on Ward's. In some years high lake water levels flood parts of the islands, closing the attractions. Whenever I visit this place, dedicated to relaxation and enjoyment, I feel an undercurrent of dislocation and desolation.

But the ferry boat to the city is always there, and I can go home anytime.

Kitchen Doors

Our grandmother's tiny kitchen was the engine of the house. And she was the engineer. Each day, she prepared breakfast, lunch, and dinner for between seven and ten people; the numbers shifted as the family dramas severed and reconfigured the living arrangements. The abrupt deposit of Tommy and me in 1953 brought that period's number in the house to eight. Our grandparents, young aunts, and uncle found themselves with a toddler and a preschooler about the house. Initially, this was a temporary arrangement. But it became apparent over time that our parents were not coming back. They had severed from each other, from us, and were somewhere unknown, patching unknown wounds in unknown ways.

The kitchen was tucked in the back corner of a World War One era house and was designed with two nearly ceiling-to-floor windows and three doors. The cookstove, icebox, and sink took up the remaining wall space. The family bought the house after World War Two and about the time we arrived made 1950s-style kitchen improvements—the installation of grey-flecked, metal-trimmed Formica counters and an enamel gas stove across the back window. A matching grey Formica table for two hugged the radiator, with a placemat-sized drop leaf, flipped up to accommodate a third person or dropped to allow walking room.

The kitchen was supported over the years by multiple deliveries. When we first arrived, the feats of the ice man entranced us. He came each week and used giant tongs to wrestle a block of ice off his horse drawn flatbed while sawdust and ice chips created a trail to the side door. Our aunts, Martha and Catherine, compared all this effort and cost with that of a refrigerator. The milk man came every few days with butter, eggs, and bottles of cream-topped milk. There was also a person known as the fruit man. Each Wednesday and Saturday at about 10:30 a.m., Sam appeared on the back stoop with a basket of fruit and vegetables for Grandma to consider.

At some point, these exchanges grew into a morning break for Sam and Grandma as well as a series of conversations that started around 1953 and ended in 1977. Grandma boiled the kettle in advance of his arrival and filled his mug with steaming water and a scoop of instant coffee. She poured the rest in the rose-patterned teapot. He took only sugar and stirred with one hand as he tucked the stubs of his two missing fingers out of sight through the cup handle. She exhaled as she sat down, taking weight off her neatly bandaged, ulcerated leg. That lesion, which had appeared during her seventh pregnancy, would never heal.

And they talked.

Most days it was just the three of us. I listened from the third chair jammed between the stove and the new refrigerator. If one of my aunts joined in, I would perch on a stepladder. I realize now that Sam was a generation younger than Grandma, but in my child's mind, they were both from the land of very old people—anyone over sixteen. Their conversations opened with the day's weather, the characteristics of the current season and predictions for the next. Storms, blights, droughts, and early frosts were discussed as well as their effect on fruits and vegetables.

"The Niagara peaches were woody last year," my grandmother noted.

"This will be a good year for the grapes," Sam observed.

Outside the tall windows, I could see the weather they were analyzing announced by the sky and the trees. Some days an insistent frigid wind unleashed a bagpipe wail through the kitchen door jam.

"There go the banshees," Grandma announced to Sam and me and added with a cheer at odds with the explanation, "It means someone has died, or soon will."

"We heard them often at the farm," she added. "And those Manitoba winds were ferocious. My mother always said it was banshees. Her parents told her that when she was little, and their parents brought the saying over from the old country."

She didn't seem at all worried by banshees, so I didn't worry. I absorbed the slow drone notes as if those preceding generations were passing only a distant sadness to me through the kitchen door.

Once Sam and Grandma had sorted out the weather and its implications, disparate anecdotes came up about life on a farm, schooling, moving to the city, the war, and their families.

Grandma described how she and the women from her village rose in the predawn to cook for field crews, whose threshers chewed across a bristling world of wheat. From a farm shack, they produced roasts, stews, potatoes, breads, pies and tanks of coffee as well as loaded tablecloth draped baskets on the horse drawn wagon three times a day for weeks during harvest. The men worked, sometimes by moonlight into the prairie night. Time was precious, the weather, capricious.

Sam talked of his boyhood farm in Italy—the lemon and orange trees, which grew on slopes, and the donkey they bought to carry bulging loads of produce. The donkey didn't seem to like Sam or work at all and without warning would stop and refuse to move. Sam pushed from behind and was kicked. A prod with a stick brought more kicks, toppling his brother. An apple worked only until the apple was gone. Sam never did succeed with that donkey. He and his brothers talked about moving to Canada. Things had to be better, and there was work, or so they had heard.

Grandma described being sent at the age of ten from her Manitoba farming village to Winnipeg on a train. By 1901, she had outstripped what the one-room schoolhouse could offer, and her parents wanted an education for her. She and a few other girls lived at a convent school where they produced Shakespeare and were examined for proficiency at keeping ledgers, darning socks, and the invisible mending of linen. Penmanship and elocution were stressed, the latter practised in formal debates on current questions, such as whether women should get the vote. She was in favour.

Sam explained the levels of schooling in Sicily. He studied mathematics, grammar, and the history of Italy, whose cities at one time had been like mighty countries. He had wanted to study further but at the age of twelve had to go to work.

It was on the first day of his first job that he lost his fingers. Sam came from a small farm and was overcome by the dirty air, yelling, and deafening equipment of the factory. He was told to clean out a machine of some kind, a smelly job that nobody else wanted. He started. Someone turned it on. At first, he felt nothing, only shock at the sight of his stubs. In time, he recovered and learned to do things without the fingers. The factory owner blamed Sam for the accident. The accusation was an injury that did not heal.

Grandma kept studying until she got a job at a Winnipeg bank. It was there that she first saw Grandad, and she added, "I gave him the glad eye." A decade later, the Depression swept them onto an eastbound train with their five children. They were almost out of money and were going to Toronto, where Grandad had a job interview.

I listened as the scarcity of food during the Second World War was described—rationing in Canada, the desperation of terrible shortages and hunger in Italy. Sam told us about the war from the vantage of a family living inside the inferno, as other countries' armies raged through their fields and homes and villages. Sam's missing fingers meant that he was far down the list of men who had to enlist in the Italian army. But another young man in his family, his cousin, had been conscripted. He didn't want to join. Sam said that almost no one in his village believed in the army or its cause. The family tried to hide his cousin by sending him away to relatives, but he was found and forced to join. Within a short time the young man was killed.

Sam's voice held outrage. Killed. For no reason.

Grandma told Sam about her eldest son, a Canadian Air Force pilot. He and his crew were killed while on night patrol over the North Sea. She talked about the things he had planned to do after the war. His body was never found. Her voice was quiet.

I learned that when Sam immigrated to Canada after World War Two, he was a labourer, and another brother worked at a fruit market. Sam thought that he might be able to make a living buying produce and selling it in parts of Toronto that lacked a nearby grocer. And he wanted to get married to Emilia who, he said, had the beauty of an angel and also had a good education, which he admired. He acquired a cart, went with his brother to the terminal before dawn, and began selling his selections on the streets of Toronto. He began getting regular customers. In time, he bought an old truck that another fruit seller no longer wanted. He could buy more produce and go further, which brought him to our street. And he married Emilia.

One morning, Grandma sent me across the street to our Aunt Mary Jo's house to ask if she wanted Grandma to buy her something from Sam. Mary

Jo hadn't been feeling well. Although she was often cheerful, she had periods where her face became grim, and she stared at others with suspicion. She shut all blinds and curtains and kept her house dark. During those episodes, we as children felt sure we had done something wrong in some great way, maybe even by just existing. This was one of those times. I knocked. Her kitchen door opened two inches, and her face glowered at me over the chain. I asked if she wanted any fruit, and she growled, "No! He charges too much."

The door banged shut.

Worry flooded me. Was Sam taking advantage of our Grandma? Were my brother and I, prodigious enjoyers of those fruits and vegetables, too much of a burden for her? The mystery of how we came to be living there caused tense looks, so we didn't ask, but we imagined explanations. And there was my aunt at her door, glaring at me about money.

On my way back, I passed Sam's turquoise truck, festooned with a cornucopia of tumbling fruits he had painted. That day it looked harsh.

"She doesn't need anything," I told Grandma and Sam.

What Aunt Mary Jo really needed, I had no idea, nor could I ask. What it all might mean shrouded the conversations I had loved.

Sometime after this I was in the kitchen with our two other aunts, and more was said about Sam's prices. Aunt Martha worked as a financial analyst, a job I didn't comprehend, and she was the family expert on money. She was smoking and talking about something called the stock market—a place where prices kept going up and down, prices that she watched every day. I asked her if Sam charged more than others.

"Why do you ask?" she wondered.

"Aunt Mary Jo said he charges too much."

She locked her pale, blue eyes on me and began a brisk tutorial on the question. She enjoyed explaining financial things, although our incomprehension astounded her. As with the many mysterious things happening around me, I stored away some of what she said to think about and hope to understand later.

She said that Sam had to pay more for produce than the larger grocers who bought in bulk. I was sure that Sam having to pay more because he could buy less, was unfair. She told me that although Sam didn't have to rent a building or pay workers, he did have to pay for his truck, gas and repairs, and "insurance coverage" —accident protection. The following day I looked over his truck and peered inside the open back doors at the crates of vegetables and fruits, the air laden with earthiness. But I could see nothing protecting it. Aunt Martha would later add that insurance was not visible and couldn't prevent bad things from happening. It was meant to help you out afterwards. But on that day, she had already moved to her final point. Although Sam did charge more than a supermarket, he provided home delivery.

"In life," she said, "you pay for services like this. Your time and effort are worth a lot. People always forget to calculate this. Especially time. Your time is very valuable."

I had to think about that.

Our other aunt, Catherine, added, "It's hard for Grandma to shop at a store. She can't walk far. But every day she has to decide what to prepare, and she knows what things cost. She has taken us all through the war, the Depression, and everyone's needs. So yes, Sam charges more. But then he brings more than fruit and vegetables to this house."

Reassurance seeped into the kitchen as the conversations about balance sheets, illuminated with what people forget to calculate, continued. It sounded like Grandma could and would always afford us. And until we grew up and went out to make our way in the world, she did.

By 1977, as Grandma lay in her upstairs bedroom in her final illness, Sam continued to come by but just once a week. My two aunts bought a little fruit they thought she'd like. He brought soup made by Emilia. Grandma's face lightened when she was told who had sent it. It was about this time that Sam scaled back and then retired his truck. He and it were showing the years. Expansive supermarkets with parking lots were absorbing much of his business.

At our Grandmother's funeral, Sam appeared with Emilia and their two daughters. All were dressed in impeccable black outfits.

My aunts Martha and Catherine kept the house, but within two years, both died of heart failure. They were still young, but their time had been cut short. My other aunt, Mary Jo, inherited and sold the old house. She entrusted the proceeds from the sale to an untrustworthy person and lost it all.

And yet.

A mysterious, nonmonetary kind of insurance, one that could never stop bad things from happening but that could help to sustain a person afterwards, had been left to me. Engendered in our grandmother's kitchen, it is with me wherever I go.

Every few years when I am in the neighbourhood, I drive by the old house. It looks much the same from the front, except for a new young tree planted. Across the back, there is now an addition that must transform the tiny old kitchen into a spacious one. Possibly the new kitchen has tightly sealed doors that better keep any banshees at bay, at least for a time.

Their song of life passing and being passed on as it's being lived.

Grandmother

My Grandmother
corseted beneath stiff layers,
bustled about in decorous rebellion
her knuckles red rough from the Monday wash.
She wanted the vote.
Now in my easy care athletic wear I run
in the cathedral of her memory.

Mary Kathryn Cassin O'Donnell

Lifelines

The snow fell all day. It smothered the road, the fields, and the farmhouse lane into undefined, undulating whiteness. It climbed the front door and heaved sideways against the deep set windows that whined complaint after resisting 120 years of winter storms. We didn't know that some of those storms had been killers. My younger brother, Tommy, and I stared out at the darkening day in hypnotized anticipation because soon we had to feed the cows up in the barn. And that meant we got to go out in a blizzard.

Our Aunt Catherine told us to batten down the barn's upper floor tractor doors once the cattle were fed. The old barn was tucked into a slope so that its lower level opened onto the front paddock, and its second storey doors were level with the higher, windier back fields. The giant tractor doors accommodated gargantuan farm equipment and teetering wagon loads. A "man door" had been cut into them to ease daily back and forth. The mammoth doors rocked and rattled in high winds. She didn't want them blown open or snow to seep under the bottom gaps, which would dampen the hay crop.

Our Aunt Catherine had been learning about these kinds of farming concerns since leaving Toronto the previous year. She and her sister, our Aunt Martha, both city dwellers in mid-life and increasingly out of shape, had purchased this farm. They had been saving a down payment for ten years, and fuelled by constant cigarettes and instant coffee, they had also been trying for ten years to stand in as parents to my brother and me.

Our actual parents had left, first one and then the other, the year we were two and four. Our perennially conversing aunts maintained an incendiary silence anywhere near this topic, seeming unable to mention their brother's name. I discovered our mother's name by overhearing their indignant fury through the kitchen door. Better not ask, we learned early on. And so we didn't know why we had landed at our grandparents' house, with our aunts in charge of us. We invented explanations that we kept to ourselves. One of these was that our heroic parents had been sent away on a secret mission by the government. Tommy had no recollection of any life before our aunts, but I, being two years older, had shards of memory, which kept me wondering if we'd be staying. About that too, I was afraid to ask.

A decade later, at ages thirteen and fifteen, we didn't question why our aunts would want to buy a farm or why they decided that Tommy would move out there with Aunt Catherine, and I would stay in Toronto with Grandma and Aunt Martha and come up every weekend and holiday. We got on with tumbling forwards on our life's mighty, unknowable currents.

On the pastel evening Mr. Andy Stuart sold the farm to our aunts, he walked us all up a hill that squatted in the back field like an improbable blimp. We scampered onto its flat summit as our aunts puffed along behind. We later learned the hill was a drumlin, ploughed into existence during the Ice Age. Mr. Stuart thought we were standing on one of the higher points of land in Erin Township.

With the sale to our aunts, Mr. Stuart would become the last of his family to live on the farm. Spread around the drumlin were a hundred acres his two times great grandparents had cleared.

In quiet phrases, he revealed what was before us. The west corner was a marshy woodlot. Beyond that was the one room schoolhouse attended by generations of his family and their neighbours' children. The north corner was stitched with twenty acres of spring corn. The east corner wrapped around a little graveyard, its scattered headstones read of long lives and the brief flickers of the short ones. Around the cemetery and everywhere beyond was a roiling sea of alfalfa, and bordering it all were dirt roads that ribboned past other farms and on into the horizon.

Mr. Stuart's ancestors had become students of this land as they laboured to define it with root fences and determine what to plant where. He explained about the purposeful placement of the barn, well, and house; the paddock, pasture, and lane; the kitchen garden; as well as the berry patches and the orchard.

As Mr. Stuart stood on the ancient drumlin speaking with open-handed steadiness, we began to understand that the long story of the past was there to be seen everywhere around us. He was introducing us to the farm and also to a way of being anchored in and illuminated by place, family, and history. The drumlin, I felt, was a place on this earth where what had been scattered and lost to me could be gathered back and recreated. As we took in the bristling fields rolling away in all directions, I knew that I was going to create an expansive future that included a sure-eyed survey of our past. An air of lightness and possibility settled within me, as heady as the alfalfa fragrance filling the evening.

For my brother and me, the drumlin would become a perpetual magnet.

The drumlin, however, was not at first in our thoughts that winter afternoon. Cows had to be fed. We trudged up the lane towards the barn. Capricious drifts had dumped snow in some places and blew the lane-way stones bare in others. To our right, the orchard trees were nodding or shaking as if in vigorous agreement and disagreement among themselves. Ahead, the black barn had become a grey hulk veiled in billowing sheets of snow.

We pushed in the narrow pass through door cut unto the tractor doors and flipped on the lights, illuminating the cathedral-like heights of the barn. It was filled past the rafters with hay bales we had stacked in midsummer, when we Toronto kids had morphed into sturdy lords of the harvest. The hay towers emanated a dusty sweetness, as if summer was still hiding out in the freezing barn.

On the lower level beneath our feet, the cows were restless, feeling the storm all around and that it was feeding time. In gentler seasons, they moseyed around the grazing pasture, but in winter, they huddled in steamy togetherness in huge indoor pens.

We cut twine to break up their dinner allotment and booted the hay through bale-sized holes cut into the floor above their feed troughs. My lanky brother scuttled monkey fast down a ladder fastened to another opening, spread feed among them, and took an axe to their ice-covered water troughs. In the past year, he had become a pint-sized authority on such matters. We stacked more bales to brace the tractor doors against the wind, which was charging at them like an infuriated bull. And we stepped outside, kicking aside drifts to latch the pass through door back in place.

The lone outdoor bulb showed flying snow and the ghostly imprimatur of the tractor path that careened around the foot of the drumlin. The end of day gave the drumlin a pale backlight, and it crouched before us as if wearing a shroud. One of us pointed up at it. Decision made. We were off to see a storm from one of the high points in Erin Township.

Since the snow went partway up our shins, we were off at a trudge, not our usual scamper. I sank up to my knees in one spot and had a flopping fight to crawl out. Deepening snow clutched every step. As the ground levelled and the going got easier, we stopped in exhausted triumph. We were on the summit. We had a lifetime of things still to learn. One of them was that going for a hike in a blizzard near the end of day wasn't wise.

Our aunt was beginning to think we were taking too long—exactly what she had told us not to do. She shoved on coat and boots and slogged up to the barn, which she found empty except for cows. They lifted their heads in mild interest but had no information other than that they looked to have been fed. It was about this time that the power failed.

She stumbled back down the shape shifting lane. Furious snow chased her through the farmhouse front door. In the brackish kitchen, she felt for flashlights, candles, and matches a-jumble in a drawer. Her breath came in sharp heaves as she hustled upstairs and stood a flashlight or candle in each of the upper window wells. This took awhile, as there were six rooms, some with two windows. In earlier times, interior doors had been installed, which divided the farmhouse into two houses to accommodate two generations of Stuart families. In winter, we lived only in the front house and left the back unlit and unheated. But this night, all upper windows of both houses shed a blondish glow.

She then headed for the far end of the back house and faced an old outer door, usually stuck shut. The first time we had shouldered it open that year, we stood on a threshold staring into the original pioneers' summer kitchen. Its dirt floor, trampled by generations of Stuarts, had sunk several feet below the rest of the farmhouse. A blackened, cavernous fireplace commanded the far wall. Here Stuart women had baked and cooked meals all day long in the warm seasons. The suffocating heat was drawn up and out through the peak of the roof, the tip of which had been removed and replaced by an open-air bell tower. Its heavy rope hung in the centre of the room. One of the women pulled it when the hefty noon dinners or evening suppers were ready, creating a voluminous "clong clang" that brought the field crews in from all around.

Our apple-shaped aunt managed the leap of several feet down to the dirt floor and then the reach up to the frozen rope. The bell tower opening filtered snow over the grey strands of her hair. She let her weight bring the rope down and hoped the old bell hinge, after all this time, was not petrified.

Up on the drumlin, we wavered in the gale. At that height, the wind was unleashed. My brother whooped. I opened my mouth to catch the stinging snow, which surged up from the ground and down from the sky, erasing any distinction between them. We twirled around in it. We lay down in it. The wildness enchanted us and lifted our souls.

We had no sense of time or danger or our aunt's worries. At ages thirteen and fifteen, a universe of stories we had yet to discover lay ahead. We didn't know that not one of the tales we'd crafted to explain our parents' absence would turn out to be right. We had yet to learn that once they shut the door on us, our parents would each go on to repeat this with their subsequent children from a succession of ruined relationships. We knew nothing of how the closing of doors would reverberate through lives.

And we knew nothing of our own ancestors, despite knowing something of the Stuarts'. We had no inkling that the same winter storm whirling about us was blanketing a pioneer cemetery in the neighbouring township and was covering the headstones of our great great-grandparents with snow. We didn't yet know their names, or that they came across ocean and through forest with their small children, desperate to get to a place of their own.

We didn't yet understand how much our aunts wanted to reignite that receding saga with a farm of their own. We hadn't lived enough years to grasp how they might have felt as young women assuming an unexpected role as our caregivers or what it is to long defer a dream or have to discard a life's direction. We didn't yet appreciate how much they wanted Tommy's scrupulous love of all living things to become deeply schooled out in the country. Or that we, through a tumble of circumstance, might have become pivotal to realizing their dream.

However, there was something we were beginning to understand up there on the drumlin. Our trek to the top had taken much longer than usual. The late afternoon light showing us the storm had sulked away. We stood in a dominion of absolute blackness—a turgid night that descends only in places remote from electric light. The snow thickened the darkness and batted our faces. Our feet could not be felt, our footprints were erased. The slicing wind came from all sides in a sightless world. Increasingly, a scalding cold was sluicing through our encrusted clothes.

I stared in each direction to find any marker of where we were. My brother laughed at the strangeness of it all. He was twirling around, scanning, but we had lost all idea of where the barn, the farmhouse, the cemetery, the cornfield, or the schoolhouse might be. I wondered, with needling panic, if we'd end up frozen somewhere by the tiny cemetery. We were surrounded by a circle of blind choices, some of which could take us into the void. But we had to pick a direction.

It was about this time that we heard it: clong clang, clong clang, clong clang. It seemed to be somewhere to our left. Seeing nothing, feet floating, and our hats heavy helmets of snowy ice, we headed towards it. We kept veering to the sound until a slight lightening revealed the hurtling snow and then the looming shape of some part of the barn. My head was hollow, disoriented. Had the barn turned itself around in the field? This was entirely a different side of the barn than I would have guessed. But it was the barn. Had a giant hand swivelled the house to face another direction? The farmhouse, each upper window beaming yellow, was not where I thought it should have been. But there it was in all its solid old warmth and grace.

Once inside the house, our aunt's recriminations were hurried because there were things to take care of, given the lack of electricity. The basement pump had to be wrapped in blankets to prevent freezing, candles and flashlights retrieved, and Sterno cans had to be found in the back house cupboard.

In the kitchen, Aunt Catherine fired up a Sterno can to heat Ovaltine, a fortification she insisted we needed after being out there so long. She began a story about a man from the area who never returned from such a walk and was discovered the next day frozen in a field.

My brother countered, "We weren't that lost."

A voice I would later grow into landed like a gavel in the room. I said, "We were well and truly lost. And since I know that, I also know that we were found."

The three of us were quiet for a moment. The only sound was the storm fighting with itself outside and the only light, a candle on the table. In the dimness, our aunt's face had the smooth prettiness I recognized from years before. But as she lit up her cigarette, I could see all the lines that had formed since, on a face radiating relief, love, and exasperation.

Over the steaming Ovaltine, I saw the face of a mother.

Aunt Catherine O'Donnell

121

Story Time

When was it, the last story I would ever read to you?

I didn't know as I turned the final page and closed the cover,
my mind on the latest hemming of a skirt, or some unpaid payment,
and put the shimmering book down.

If I had only known it was the last time.

I would have lingered with you my child in the kingdom spread before us
to slay dragons and walk the castle gardens
and challenge every crooked style.

But, of course, I did not know.

And now you venture forth to uncharted lands
made in the memories I am losing
as I stand on tiptoe to kiss you goodbye.

Acknowledgements

This collection of memoirs has been carefully and lovingly mothered and nurtured by many people to bring it to maturity. The authors would like to offer their sincere thanks to the many friends and acquaintances who played a part in making it a reality.

A huge thank you:

To the Academy for Lifelong Learning, Toronto, where we all met many years ago in various workshops, until Brenda Doyle brought this group together to write about mothers and mothering.

To Teresa Poulton for her attentive editing.

To Mindy Johnstone for her beautiful artwork.

To Axel Peter von Bertoldi for his endless hours on layout and typesetting.

Each of us called on various friends and family members as we drafted and revised the pieces here.

Brenda thanks her husband, Peter, as well as the other members of this collective for their support and encouragement.

Nancy thanks Judy Turner for her long-time support and encouragement and her sister Lynn for her loving validation.

Kathy thanks Brenda, Ellen, Jennifer, Melanie, and Nancy for their generous encouragement. She thanks her children, Asher and Lara, whose lives gave hers meaning. She thanks Lorne, her soulmate of forty-five years, for making sure she laughs every day. Finally, she thanks the many, extraordinary women, alive and deceased, with whom she had the privilege to cross paths and who fanned the flames of inspiration, especially Alexandra Brody and her mother, Nina Cambell, who to this day she catches herself wanting to call for advice.

Melanie thanks her husband, Doug Reeve, for reading and editing innumerable drafts and for his love and support through every insecure and self-doubting moment.

Jennifer thanks Jane Allen for valuable information, her sister, Betty, for her loving support as well as the other members of this team.

Ellen thanks her husband, Don, and children, Cecily, Dominic, and Emily for their encouragement as well as their technical and creative help, and her brother Tom for sharing a trunkful of recollections.

Deepest appreciation to
Demeter's monthly Donors

DEMETER

Daughters
Rebecca Bromwich
Summer Cunningham
Tatjana Takseva
Debbie Byrd
Fiona Green
Tanya Cassidy
Vicki Noble
Naomi McPherson
Myrel Chernick

Sisters
Amber Kinser
Nicole Willey
Christine Peets